*security* TRANSFORMATION

**Also co-authored by Mary Pat McCarthy**

*Digital Transformation: The Essentials of e-Business Leadership*

# security TRANSFORMATION

### Digital Defense Strategies to Protect Your Company's Reputation and Market Share

*Mary Pat McCarthy*
*Stuart Campbell*

*with Rob Brownstein*

McGraw-Hill

New York   Chicago   San Francisco   Lisbon
London   Madrid   Mexico City   Milan
New Delhi   San Juan   Seoul
Singapore   Sydney   Toronto

## McGraw-Hill

*A Division of The McGraw·Hill Companies*

2 3 4 5 6 7 8 9 0 DOC/DOC 0 9 8 7 6 5 4 3 2 1

ISBN 0-07-137966-5

Printed and bound by R.R. Donnelley & Sons

 This book is printed on recycled, acid-free paper containing a minimum of 50% recycled, de-inked fiber.

# Contents

## PART V: PEERING AHEAD

# Foreword

For as long as humankind has existed, security has been a primary concern. Until recently, the focus was largely on physical security: Is my family safe? Is there a secure supply of food? Do I have shelter? But in the past few decades, the computer age has got us all thinking about security for our personal and business information, and the Internet has magnified those concerns. In an era when it seems that almost every byte of data about our lives is but a few clicks away, will we ever be confident that this information is secure?

Such fears will likely increase, because we are only at the dawn of the Internet age. Today, most of our interactions with the Internet involve simple email or viewing Web pages. The next-generation Internet will make 2001 seem like the digital Stone Age. Computers will collaborate over the Internet to gather data on our behalf, and do that with little help from us. Our homes and all the appliances in them will also be online, quietly deciding what needs servicing, ordering, or replacing, and organizing the appropriate actions and payment. When you schedule a hospital appointment, your insurer, physician, and personal calendar will automatically be notified. Your entire life, at one level, will be lived on the Net.

This isn't science fiction: It will be a reality for many of us within a few years, one that will bring incredible benefits in personal productivity, efficiency, and quality of life. But as we live more of our lives online, we put more of our personal data at risk. How significant that risk will be is a factor of how well we design the processes and technologies that will protect us. I truly believe that the rewards of the digital age far surpass its risks, and that we have it in our power to effectively manage what hazards do lie there.

To succeed, however, we need to take a new approach to computer systems and the underlying critical information infrastructure. We are increasingly overwhelmed by the scale and complexity of computer systems. We need to learn new ways to specify, design, implement, manage, and audit those systems—to get to a point where the computers themselves are more directly involved in those roles, rather than simply "coded and administered" as they are today.

This book challenges readers to think about information security in new ways, and to crystallize the range of risks to the information infrastructure—risks that could threaten everything from personal data to the nation's money, water, and power supplies. That approach goes beyond the traditional risk-management view to explore the benefits security technology can provide—strategies that can enhance customer value, enable new business opportunities, protect brands, and help companies avoid liability.

Microsoft's vision is to empower people through great software—any time, any place, and on any device. That pushes us to look outside the technological box for creative new solutions. This book challenges you to look at information security in the same way—to consider solutions that extend beyond the technological to include vision, people, and entirely new ways of doing business.

Craig Mundie
Senior Vice President, Advanced Strategies
Microsoft Corporation
March 2001

# Acknowledgments

We are extremely grateful for the generous contributions of the many business leaders who agreed to be interviewed for this book. These include Michael Capellas, John Charters, Gary Dilts, Ellen Hancock, George Keyworth, Rhonda MacLean, William Malik, Terry Milholland, Craig Mundie, Peter Rosamilia, Richard Sarnoff, Howard Schmidt, Stratton Sclavos, Mark Walsh, and Peter Weiss. Their thoughtful commentary and perspective added greatly to our knowledge and to the quality of this book. Our partners Brian Ambrose, Barbara Carbone, Mark Carleton, Kevin Coleman, Glen Davison, James Devaul, Bradley Fisher, Carl Geppert, Larry Kelsey, Shahed Latif, Danny Le, Mark Lindig, Robert Litt, Gary Lord, Jack Miller, Tom Moser, Gene O'Kelly, Michael O'Malley, Tim Pearson, Gary Riske, Ed Rodriguez, Greg Russo, Ron Safran, Terri Santisi, Ted Senko, Frank Taylor, Henry Teng, and Al Van Ranst played a major role in shaping our thoughts and supporting our efforts. We are also thankful to Marie Glenn, our editor, for her contribution and commitment and to Eric Fisch for his valuable assistance. You prove that there is indeed security in numbers. And security is what this book is all about. Thank you.

Mary Pat McCarthy
Stuart Campbell
March 2001

# Introduction

I s it safe? Is the Internet a safe neighborhood for e-commerce and e-business? Well, that depends. In any neighborhood, some houses and some cars are safer than others. Professional thieves do their homework and hit those places that are least protected. Even an amateur thief will avoid the obvious and steal a car without a steering-wheel locking bar, or break into a house that has no alarm system or barking dog.

So the real issue isn't whether the Internet is safe; it's whether your enterprise and its Web presence are safe. And that's the challenge. A secure enterprise environment must address both neighborhoods—the network neighborhood as well as the physical neighborhood. How effective is an iron-clad network security system if someone can easily enter your facility, sit down at a network-connected computer, and download sensitive information? Yet, you would be surprised at how often the opportunities occur for doing just that.

Taking a different perspective, what level of security does your business really require? For companies involved in electronic fund transfers, there's one answer; for companies selling books over the Web, there's another. For institutions and medical centers exchanging patient records over the Net, there are privacy issues. For companies holding customer credit card information, there are theft issues. And what about major automobile manufacturers who intend to streamline their supplier relationships through a common Web entity? How secure must that entity be in order to protect intellectual property, bid information, and other facets critical to competition?

Clearly, every company is unique, even those in the same industry. They have unique locations, personnel, brands, reputations, products, and customers. Could Amazon or eBay have been enabled without security? What about E*Trade? Would Intel's or Cisco's customers and suppliers have joined them in their e-business transformations without appropriate security? In all of these cases, security was an enabler that allowed those companies to expand their businesses and lower their operating costs.

**With unlimited time and an unlimited budget, you can build a nearly perfect security environment. In a relatively short time, with a realistic budget, you can build an appropriate security environment.**

What are your company's biggest threats? What are your vulnerabilities? What assets do they affect, and what's the exposure? The answers to these questions constitute your risk profile, and you need to understand what that risk is in order to intelligently define and establish an appropriate enterprise security environment.

This book looks at the whole enterprise with regard to enterprise security. It details the kinds of methods and tools available for assessing security vulnerabilities, and methods used for looking beyond your current security environment to one that will serve your present and future needs in the most scalable and least disruptive way.

With unlimited time and an unlimited budget, you can build a nearly perfect security environment. In a relatively short time, with a realistic budget, you can build an appropriate security environment. This book will help you understand what you need to do.

No one likes to describe his or her company as "reactive." We all like to feel "proactive." There are times, though, when reaction is the only card we have to play. This, however, isn't one of them. If you have the means to check, we're sure your enterprise has been "attacked." Many attacks may have been inadvertent, but it's likely several were the purposeful rattling of doorknobs and windows. One survey reported that 90 percent of respondents detected cyber attacks on their systems in the last 12 months. And financial losses from 273 of those surveyed topped $265 million. If your enterprise has never been breached, consider yourself lucky. But the odds are great that it will happen in the future.

You need to raise the bar on prevention of both remote and local intrusion. You need to increase the effectiveness and speed of intrusion detection, and integrate the technology with the people who have the responsibility. And, you need to put in place an effective response that can mitigate disruption or damage, identify intrusion aftereffects, and remedy them. If you do all of that, and do it well, your answer to the question, "Is it safe?" will be, "Yes."

# PART I

# Are You Scared Yet?

# CHAPTER 1

# The World under Siege

One early April morning in 1997, the presidents of the United States, Russia, and France; and the prime ministers of the United Kingdom, Japan, and Canada all received an email message. It was a blackmail message.

"Every major computer system in the world has been infected with an undetectable 'logic bomb.' On a specific date and time, all of these bombs will go off, and the entire world's systems dependent on computer control will crash. As proof, we will offer a small demonstration of our abilities on May 1, 1997 at 00:00 UTC. After that, we will contact you all again." The email message appeared to come from a well-known ISP, and the user name was "Alpha."

In the ensuing three weeks, the U.S. Secret Service determined that the message origination address was "spoofed" (or had been replaced by a phony address). A cursory query to IT managers of government systems and a few large, private-sector systems showed no indication of unauthorized access. By April 24, the U.S. government had written off the email message as a hoax.

At precisely 00:00 UTC on May 1, 1997, a major computer-controlled radar center near Denver, responsible for tracking high-altitude commercial aircraft traffic, suddenly froze. Radar screens stopped flashing, and within seconds, the flights being tracked disappeared off them. Air traffic controllers scrambled to alert the pilots and contingency procedures were quickly put in place.

Long before any of the media could broadcast news about the incident, Alpha had sent another email to the U.S. President. "It's hard to track airliners without radar, isn't it? We'll be in touch. Alpha."

Within days, dozens of experts were poring over the system software used in that Denver radar facility. Meanwhile, the President called together his national security team to brief them on the emails and their connection with the radar failure.

WHITE HOUSE OPERATIONS ROOM, MAY 11, 1997

*"As far as we know, the Denver incident was the only incident," said the Secretary of Defense. "We've held informal briefings with our counterparts in the other countries that received the email, and they've reported nothing unusual for now."*

*"What have we found in Denver?" asked a national security specialist.*

*"So far, we've come up empty," said the Secretary.*

*"Have they discovered where the email came from?" asked another national security person.*

*"Nope. The senders covered their tracks very well," the Secretary replied.*

*"What do you think the Alpha group plans to do?" the President interjected.*

*"It has all the earmarks of a blackmail gambit," said the FBI Director, who had also been invited. "The first email established the threat, the Denver incident proved they meant business, and the next message is likely to be the blackmail payoff message," he added.*

By the time the meeting had concluded, a team made up of security, software, and crime experts had been assembled and assigned full-time to the Alpha Project, as it was called. One team member provided liaison with the other teams being assembled in London, Moscow, Paris, Toronto, and Tokyo.

Because the threat implied it would affect worldwide systems, the six heads of state agreed it would be politic to inform the United Nations and, thereby, all the other countries of the world. Meanwhile, experts continued to scrutinize the radar system's code.

Two days after they had begun combing through the software, one of the software experts suggested they compare it to the last version that had been backed up before the incident. When they did, they found the "bomb." It was an innocuous-looking piece of code, triggered by the date and time. When triggered, it would cause the system to crash after it executed a small set of instructions; the last instruction was to erase the code itself, leaving only a slight modification to the date and time trigger.

With the culprit under the microscope—assuming it was the template for the other bombs that Alpha had claimed were already in place—the team had something for which to search.

The national security group had debated whether to share this finding with the whole Alpha Project team; the consensus was to freely distribute the information because there was no proof that the Alpha action was politically motivated. In fact, they decided to share that new information with the world and used the United Nations as the dissemination agent.

Within a week there were experts in more than two dozen countries combing through code 24 hours per day. The team in the U.S. had so far found no further instances of the Denver code in any of the software they'd examined. Reports from other countries indicated no one else had found any, either.

On a Friday near the end of May, the other shoe dropped. The email message read: "By now you've discovered our Denver 'bomb' and have no doubt searched for others like it. Don't waste your time. You won't find any. If you want to know what the other logic bomb is like, it will cost you $100 billion in cash. Otherwise, on December 31, 1997 at 00:00 UTC, 'poof.'" The message, as before, was signed "Alpha."

By then the coordinated efforts of all the countries' teams had turned up no further suspect code. And the heads of state of the original six countries had all received the black-mail message. Each of these countries appointed two representatives to the Alpha Project team to decide on subsequent steps.

Even as the project team met, Alpha sent another message. "In order for you to safely defuse the logic bomb, you will need our information no later than October 31, 1997. Therefore, if you intend to pay us our consulting fee of $100 billion, you will need to arrange to deliver our funds, and do so by October 1, 1997. That will give us sufficient time to give you the information you will need, and for you to use that information to avoid a worldwide catastrophe. If you agree to our terms, let us know on August 1, 1997." The message concluded with the address of a well-known bulletin board and instructions to simply post a "Yes, Alpha" message to that board on August 1.

WHITE HOUSE OPERATIONS ROOM, MAY 30, 1997
*"What if there are no other bombs?" asked the Secretary. "What if the only bomb was the one in Denver, and he's bluffing about the others?"*

*"And what if he's not?" countered the President. "Can we really take the chance?"*

*"Look, we've already searched through about one billion lines of code and we haven't found anything strange," the Secretary replied.*

*"I recommend we continue examining mission-critical code until we hear from Alpha again," said a national security expert. "There's just too much risk in assuming we're dealing with a hoax."*

*The Secretary then motioned to an assistant who darkened the room lights, switched on a projector, and put up a slide showing the estimates of lines of code broken down by individual government areas, such as air traffic control.*

*"Gentlemen, we're not even sure of what we're looking for," he began, "but even if we were, the amount of code we would have to examine is mind-boggling. I'd argue that even if Alpha gave us the code, we would be hard-pressed to find and defuse it in time."*

*He signaled for the next slide and explained, "Here is the estimated number of man-years and costs associated with a line-by-line examination of just the code we delineated on the previous slide. This does not touch, at all, on private sector programs that could affect our national infrastructure, such as programs controlling electronic funds transfers. I believe we're engaged in nothing short of a latter-day Manhattan Project, and the costs may eclipse those for sending a man to the Moon."*

*One of the national security experts interjected, "At least, the private sector will have to pay its own way," and several people snickered.*

*"This isn't about costs, gentlemen," said the President. "This is about national catastrophe. This is about life imitating art. It's like that movie,* **The Day the Earth Stood Still,** *but the motive isn't benevolent, and the duration is unpredictable."*

The meeting ended with a decision to continue examining the government's system and application codes while waiting for Alpha's next message. It took 10 days.

"This is a bit like a chess game, isn't it? You've looked for a code like the one in Denver and come up dry. Now you're wondering if there is no other code. Some of you are willing to take that chance; some of you are not. Well, my assuring you of our serious intent is insufficient. So, another example is required. On July 4, at precisely 00:00 UTC, there will be fireworks. Then, we will get down to business. I'll contact you, all, again on July 5 with the specifics. Alpha."

WHITE HOUSE OPERATIONS ROOM, JUNE 10, 1997

*"What the heck do they mean by 'fireworks?'" the Secretary began. "The last demonstration resulted in no casualties. This one sounds more ominous."*

*"We'll have to assume this demonstration will be more dramatic, so let's alert the U.N. and the national transportation infrastructure about the risks associated with that date and time," said the FBI Director.*

*"And let's hope that whatever happens is dramatic enough to suit Alpha's purpose but puts no one's life at risk," the President said soberly.*

The tension mounted as the clock ticked inexorably toward July 4. Airlines rescheduled flights to ensure no planes were in the air at 00:00 UTC on that date. Railroads rescheduled their trains to keep them out of service at that time.

But Alpha's demonstration had nothing to do, directly, with planes or trains. On July 4, at 00:00 UTC, a Northeastern U.S. power utility control computer, that automatically switches power sources in response to varying load demands, created a massive short circuit at a major power distribution station. The result was a fireworks display that rivaled the best of the municipal celebrations scheduled for later that day. And it triggered a massive power blackout in Massachusetts and New Hampshire.

Again, the code was examined with a fine-tooth comb. And, again, the code showed no evidence of tampering. As before, by comparing the program to a backed up, pre-incident version, the experts discovered a small, date-and-time triggered interrupt program, which called a subroutine that set up the short circuit. As before, the code erased both itself and that subroutine.

A pattern was emerging. In both demonstrations a date and time triggered the event. And, in both demonstrations, the code was self-erasing. The question was, when had the code originally been inserted? The answer, found by comparing earlier backed-up versions that revealed some slight tampering, was during the second week of April in 1996.

That time period coincided with a routine maintenance and upgrade of the program by a service contractor. This would have been an opportune time for new code to be inserted, and apparently that's exactly what happened.

From July 6 until October 1, the Alpha Project people compiled a list of 500 government and private sector systems that would be likely targets for a coordinated shut-down of the United States' telecommunications, financial, power generation and distribution, and travel infrastructures. The latter included fully automated systems such as California's Bay Area Rapid Transit (BART), connecting San Francisco with points south and east, and New York City's subway system.

Having identified this list, they began a systematic examination of programs prior to and just after routine maintenance or upgrade services. Within days they discovered logic bombs in 25 separate programs, each like the ones used in the prior two incidents.

In some cases, system backups prior to maintenance and service intervals had already been erased, adding to the difficulty of comparing the current systems. But little by little, the modus operandi emerged and telltale code trails became apparent. Using these clues, 100 more programs yielded their hidden booby traps.

It was decided that the project team would play along with Alpha, and proceed with an apparent commitment to meet Alpha's demands. In that way, the team hoped to prevent Alpha from executing a "plan B" effort and, at the same time, give the intelligence services more time to try to find Alpha.

At the same time, information about the logic bombs was disseminated quickly within the U.N. Security Council to allow other countries to identify similar code objects. By September 20, 1997, logic bombs had been discovered and defused in 206 of the 500 suspect programs. None had been discovered outside the U.S.

Security procedures for all 500 systems were severely tightened to prevent unauthorized access to the programs, and no further emails were received from Alpha. The remaining 294 programs were being examined 24 hours a day right up until December 31, 1997 at 00:00 UTC. At the stroke of midnight, 12 programs among the remaining 294 crashed. They caused blackouts in New Orleans and St. Paul, the failure of Miami's monorail system, a partial freeze of the air traffic control system at La Guardia Airport in New York, and the derailment of an Amtrak train near Chicago. No one was killed. No planes crashed. The infrastructure survived.

. . .

The preceding story is fiction, but not far-fetched. In fact, the world was under siege in the late 1990s, but the villains were not terrorists. They were all the programmers who, since the 1950s, had used two-digit year fields in system and applications software.

Without question, a lot has been written about the so-called Y2K bug. And a lot of money was spent in response to it—estimated to be between $600 and $800 billion. Some argue that it was a tempest in a teapot; others were hoarding food and water as the new millennium approached.

With enough people digging into the history of the problem, it was inevitable that one person would be identified and given the dubious distinction of being called responsible. That person, Robert Berner, worked for IBM in the

1950s, and developed the alternative two-digit field for recording years.

In fairness to Berner, he pointed out the consequences of the two-digit year field decision. He did it in the 1950s and he did it again in 1970. In fact, in 1970, he had the support of almost 90 respected scientists and well-known technical organizations in his argument to Edward David, then President Nixon's science adviser. Obviously, his warning went unheeded.

But the year field was never the real problem. Denial was. It took nearly three decades to elevate the potential problem to the necessary level of consciousness before companies and governments began taking action. And by then, according to Peter de Jager, an early voice of alarm, there was really no time to attack the whole problem. Instead, business and government task forces engaged in what Jager described as an embarrassing effort of "triage." They tried to identify the really crucial areas of vulnerability and focused all their efforts on these—finance, transportation, communications, and power industries—critical threads of our global, social fabric.

> **The year field was never the real problem. Denial was.**

We contend that the Y2K saga was predictable. Given 30 years to ponder a problem, people tend to slip it under the "to do" stack. It was only the approaching trigger date that stirred things into action.

> **We contend that the Y2K saga was predictable. Given 30 years to ponder a problem, people tend to slip it under the "to do" stack.**

What if Nixon had listened to Berner in 1970? What if we had stopped writing code with two-digit year fields then? Would the incremental cost of the additional two characters, in terms of additional storage, additional keypunch labor, and the like, have added up to $600 to $800 billion dollars over 30 years? We think not.

But what would have happened if no one had raised an alarm? A hole in the ozone might have looked tame compared to the unpredictable behavior of thousands of system and applications programs, worldwide.

The Y2K episode is an example of a proactive response to a potential threat. True, the response came rather late in the game, but it preceded the disaster to which it was responding. Would it have been preferable to do nothing until January 1, 2000, and then begin reacting to what could have been myriad upsets in those key threads of the global social fabric—finance, transportation, communications, and power industries? In that case, the response would have been post-disaster, and we would have been frantically trying to fix things amid the likely chaos of money transfer, air travel, telephone, network, and electrical disruptions. We would argue that the ultimate cost would have been much higher, and the social costs potentially unimaginable.

By taking the action we did, late as it was, we were limiting our risks in advance. If there were going to be disruptions on January 1, 2000, at least we were able to lower that risk in areas considered critical. That is something you can do when you plan and execute ahead of an event, and it is the primary reason we recommend so strongly taking a proactive approach to computer security.

Security vulnerabilities are real and they will never be reduced to zero. Prevention can be strengthened, but it will never be absolute. There is a definite advantage to taking steps before rather than after an attack. Even then, unpleasant things happen.

If you're still wondering about the seriousness of Y2K, consider these post-millennium reports. There were more than 100 significant failures in January 2000 alone, with 67 occurring in the first week. Failures were reported in nuclear power plants; even a military spy satellite went blank for a while.

Among the reported incidents in London's *The Independent* were the following:

- ❏ Seven U.S. nuclear plants experienced "minor problems."
- ❏ Two nuclear power plants in Japan had "failures."
- ❏ French military satellites "lost" data.
- ❏ Cash and credit cards issued by U.S. banks could not be validated.
- ❏ U.S. Medicare payments were disrupted.
- ❏ Traffic lights in Jamaica failed.
- ❏ Customer records at a foreign bank in Japan were deleted.
- ❏ A customer returning a rented videotape was charged $91,000 for being 100 years late!

We will never know what might have happened if we had simply left things to chance on January 1, 2000. And that's good.

# CHAPTER 2

# Just When We Thought It Was Safe ...

On January 1, 2000, the world sighed in collective relief that its financial, telecommunications, and power distribution facilities had not stopped working because of the so-called Y2K bug.

Four weeks later, as Y2K was rapidly dimming in peoples' memories, a three-day series of events shattered our placidity. It started on Monday, February 7. Yahoo.com became inaccessible for several hours. The next day, Buy.com, Amazon.com, eBay.com, and CNN.com suffered similar symptoms. And on Wednesday, ZDNet.com and E*Trade.com were struck.

The cause of the cyber malaise was something called a "distributed denial of service" or DDoS attack. It was akin to hundreds of people trying to call an "800" number at the same time—virtually no one gets through. But it wasn't the work of hundreds of people. It was the work of one person.

We don't know his real name. The Canadian government does not release the names of criminals under 16 years of age. The lad from Montreal was known to a select, small Internet circle as "Mafiaboy," and on January 18, 2001, he pled guilty to 56 charges stemming from his activities almost one year before.

Keep in mind that Mafiaboy *did not penetrate* the secure Web sites of Yahoo and the others; he just made it impossible for anyone else to gain access to those sites. No credit card accounts were copied, no data was altered, and no trade secrets were pilfered. Yet, his three-day exploit may have cost those companies several millions of dollars in lost revenue, customers, and reputation.

Two weeks later, Microsoft's and National Discount Brokers' Web sites also came under attack. Even the FBI's Web site was subjected to a denial of service (DoS) attack, as was RSA.com, the Web site for RSA Security, a leading provider of Internet encryption technology. Was it Mafiaboy, or copycats? It really doesn't matter.

Mafiaboy was a 15-year-old with too much time on his hands. Called "script kiddies," hundreds of juveniles, with no real understanding of what they're doing and how it works, have access to serious hacking tools and procedures, often freely distributed on a variety of Web sites. Sometimes their attacks are as easily launched as typing in a URL and pushing a button.

## ALL ATTACKS ARE NOT EQUAL

While the media loves to lump all Internet attacks under one broad category, attacks differ in methods and effects. Some involve network penetration; others do not. Some involve tampering or theft; others interfere with normal Web site operation. But all are illegal.

### Annoyance and Loss

DoS and DDoS attacks are not about privacy contravention, data corruption, or theft. They are about widespread disruptions of service and the losses that follow in their wake. These are the attacks that have gotten the most press, and these are the attacks to which virtually every Web site is most at risk. Does your company derive revenue from online trans-

> **DoS and DDoS attacks are not about privacy contravention, data corruption, or theft. They are about widespread disruptions of service and the losses that follow in their wake.**

actions? What are your losses when Web site activity is hampered or suspended?

### Breaking and Entering

Compromising privacy, playing havoc with data, and stealing all mean someone has gained access to a system. In June and July 2000, someone gained access to confidential medical information at the University of Washington's Medical Center. That person used the Internet to gather thousands of files filled with names, conditions, addresses, and Social Security numbers.

How was it done? The attacker, working through a public Web site, planted a "sniffer" (a software program that works in conjunction with a network interface card) and got the ID and password of a legitimate user of the University of Washington system. Then, he or she used that ID and password to access two databases containing over 4,000 patient records.

In this case, the intruder meant only to show the holes in the security of that system. But the information could have been used in a variety of illegal ways. There are definite advantages to having patient information online. It allows doctors and hospitals to quickly and inexpensively share that information. But fears about unauthorized record access could inhibit an otherwise efficient, cost-cutting practice.

Has your network been broken into? Would you know? What secrets have been examined? What secret ways have been left behind to make subsequent visits that much easier?

## Penetration and Theft

During the summer of 1998, a computer consultant stole a laptop computer from Sprint, and two accomplices made off with the passwords of several Sprint employees. Using the laptop and the passwords, the trio were able to penetrate Sprint's network and gain access to the cell phone accounts payable records. It was a relatively simple matter to then mark "paid" over $2 million in cell phone bills. Sprint was out $2 million, some customers were ahead nearly $2 million, and the trio were paid a commission. Have your accounts receivable records been altered? Would you know?

More recently, someone broke into Egghead.com's computer system. For several days there was great concern that the credit card accounts of nearly 3.5 million customers may have been stolen. In any case, Egghead responded quickly by emailing its customer list to inform them about the break-in. Some credit card companies automatically cancelled some of those accounts. When Egghead later announced that, in fact, the credit card information had not been compromised, it was too late. Many users had already canceled their cards, in addition to those that had been automatically canceled for them. No one was pleased. And if, indeed, the card information had been stolen and put to fraudulent use, would Egghead have been held liable? Are you legally responsible for information you hold? If so, what's your exposure?

## EVEN THE PENTAGON GETS ATTACKED

Ikenna Iffih was a 28-year-old student at Northeastern University's College of Computer Science. He recently pleaded guilty to a hacking spree of military and government networks that had given him control over a NASA computer system.

In case you're wondering, Iffih's work wasn't an isolated case. The Defense Department counted more than 22,000 electronic attacks against its systems during 1999. Most, according to the Defense Department, were harmless annoyances. Some, though, were believed to be the work of hackers in foreign countries. And some of those intruders were able to break into Pentagon computer systems and download large amounts of unclassified (albeit not public) information.

Pentagon officials added that to the best of their knowledge, their classified computer systems had not been breached. Now, keep in mind that the Defense Department has about 10,000 computer systems and 1.5 million individual computers. About 2,000 of those systems are mission-critical. In 1999, the Department detected more than 22,000 attempts to probe, scan, penetrate, or disseminate viruses. About three percent (600 or more) of those attempts resulted in temporary shutdowns or other system disruptions. So, where do you keep your classified information? What is it worth to you and your company?

**The Defense Department counted more than 22,000 electronic attacks against its systems during 1999.**

## VIRUSES AND TROJAN PROGRAMS

Another thing to keep in mind is that computer crime isn't a new phenomenon. In 1989, a graduate student, Robert Morris, unleashed what might have been the Internet's first virus. In January 1994, Trojan programs had been implanted in several Internet-connected computers. These innocuous-looking programs purport to do one thing but actually do something else. In this case, what they did was monitor network traffic and capture user names and passwords. The federally funded Computer Emergency Response Team (CERT) released an advisory saying that people employing advanced surveillance software were illicitly collecting thousands of passwords. The advisory added that illegal collection was probably continuing and increasing. (This proved to be prophetic.) Does your network have a Trojan program lurking on it? Would you know?

## SOMEONE ELSE'S VULNERABILITY BECOMES YOUR PROBLEM

In 1999, Microsoft elected to temporarily shut down its Hotmail service when it discovered that intruders were able to read the emails of its more than 50 million subscribers. Hotmail had been acquired by Microsoft with its security mechanisms already in place. Hackers in Britain and Sweden publicized a nine-line code that could circumvent that security. That made it hot mail, indeed.

"That's one of the dangers as companies acquire or merge with others," said Terry Milholland, chief information officer and chief technology officer at EDS. "Often, when a new company is acquired, you know very little about their level of security. Yet, your job is still to bring them into the fold; and the more difficult the integration, the greater the risk potential that something downstream will compromise the security of the whole system."

## SO, NO ONE'S SAFE, RIGHT?

We could certainly write an entire book about just the last few years' worth of Internet "incidents." In fact, we could write several books. The point is, they happen. They can happen to anyone—even the CIA! (The CIA discovered a secret chat room on its network that had been operating for over five years.) But while they may not be new, they do have a negative impact on everyone's perception of Internet safety.

If there's so much insecurity on the Net, why do people use it? Because the Internet offers amazing opportunities for creating new business models, achieving new levels of efficiency, and establishing seamless alliances and partnerships. Yet, the very same features that enable all these benefits—ubiquity, speed, worldwide connectivity, platform independence—create the opportunities for mischief, fraud, and larceny.

## INTERNET STRENGTHS

The Internet as a channel for trade and a foundation for new business models is still very new—and exciting. In the book *Digital Transformation* (McGraw-Hill, 2000), authors Patel and McCarthy described the opportunities for enhanced competitiveness, lowered operating costs, faster order-to-delivery times, and partnering that today's Web affords us.

The Web's standards-based, platform-independent characteristics removed many of the obstacles to electronic data interchange (EDI). It also lowered many of the barriers to international communications, and enhanced global commerce. The ability of companies to use the Internet as a means of quickly building integrated alliances has certainly speeded up business reaction rates. And the Web has been a factor in the creation of new businesses and business models.

## INTERNET SUSCEPTIBILITIES

The Web is a public network. That means sensitive information is exchanged in an inherently non-secured environment. By taking advantage of the Web's connectivity, companies are also increasing the number of "ways in" to their enterprise networks. Before the days of virtual private networks (VPNs), there were actual private networks, and intruders needed to work from inside. With the Internet connected to proxy servers, firewalls, and intranets, it is now possible for someone half a world away to tamper with a company's information.

As progress continues in wireless networks and wireless Internet access, data is now traveling as radio waves. Remember some of the scandalous cell phone conversations picked up by unintended listeners using radio scanners? Then, you recognize the added vulnerabilities of data transfers unbounded by wired connections.

The standards-based nature of the Internet is a key to its ubiquity. It is also its Achilles' heel. The Transmission Control Protocol/ Internet Protocol (TCP/IP) was never intended as a security-ori-

**The standards-based nature of the Internet is a key to its ubiquity. It is also its Achilles' heel.**

ented protocol, yet the pair underlies virtually every Internet data transfer. Well-publicized Web operating systems make it easier for engineers to develop applications for them. But operating systems left in default configurations also present an opportunity for mischief, or worse. "Holes" in such programs have been well studied and described. When a potential intruder finds a default-configured operating system (OS), the path to entry is already well marked.

Using proprietary security mechanisms is no guarantee of tamper-free operation, either. At least public domain security schemes are open to thorough testing and disclosure. A proprietary approach that has been breached, on the other hand, may escape public disclosure. As a result, it will remain vulnerable to assault while its user companies remain confident in its prevention characteristics.

## CONTINUING E-BUSINESS GROWTH

Despite the DoS attacks in February 2000, and the more recent incidents, e-business is continuing to grow and prosper. Intel's e-business, for example, relies upon tight security. As Patel and McCarthy pointed out, without an amply large encryption scheme, Intel and its partners would have lacked confidence in the Web's ability to keep their shared information secure.

For its part, Cisco has created a seamless manufacturing environment made up of a few Cisco manufacturing sites and dozens of alliance partner sites. Here again, information security is paramount. Security is also a key enabler of Cisco's ability to create partnerships quickly in pursuit of rapidly emerging opportunities.

As Ford, General Motors, and DaimlerChrysler await the launch of their Covisint exchange, they believe it will be possible to provide the necessary security that can enable fierce competitors and their network of suppliers to share that exchange. "Just look at the financial services industry," says Gary Dilts, senior vice president of e-Connect Platform with DaimlerChrysler Corporation. "I'm not worried about buying securities or doing banking transactions online. They've proven it can be done, and I believe we will achieve it with Covisint."

## SECURITY AS AN ENABLER

It is important to recognize that for Intel, Cisco, and the Big Three automakers, security is an enabler, not an inhibitor. It provides the assurance needed to conduct their business without placing obstacles in front of their alliance partners. This is an important point, because in choosing a security environment one can go too far and end up inhibiting rather than enhancing one's business.

For example, some stores have security environments in which customers select merchandise from a catalog, fill out a slip, pay for the goods, and then use the invoice marked "paid" as the means for receiving the merchandise. The advantage, of course, is that customers never put their hands on the goods until after they have been paid for. The disadvantage, though, is that some customers are wary about buying things they can't look at and try out.

Other stores deal with that problem by tagging merchandise with removable security tags. Customers can handle the goods, but unless they are paid for, the tags remain in place and will trigger an alarm should the customer try to remove those articles from the store.

Virtually every store could beef up its security much further, but there is a definite point of diminishing returns, after which additional security becomes an inhibitor rather than an enabler of business.

With regard to the Internet, there is certainly no shortage of security solutions being touted. This is all right, so long as the implication is treatment rather than cure. Often, the term *security solution* suggests the security risk has been eliminated. Nothing could be further from the truth. Not one single security solution has ever proven to be perfectly secure. And, for a variety of reasons, none ever will. All solutions are relative.

> **Not one single security solution has ever proven to be perfectly secure. And, for a variety of reasons, none ever will. All solutions are relative.**

## RELATIVE SOLUTIONS

A relative solution is based on a real assessment of vulnerabilities and exposure. It balances the cost of security against a worst-case loss scenario. Its objectives are driven by a real, activity-based analysis of transactions and data. And it is always a combination of objectives, people, procedures, and tools. It's never perfect, but a well-crafted security environment enhances legitimate business practices while deterring the illegitimate. The time to put one in place is before—not after—a serious attack. And that environment should be flexible enough to accommodate changing needs.

## BECOMING PROACTIVE

Let's be honest. Humankind has never been known for proaction. We wait until the atmosphere gets too warm before making serious attempts at air pollution reduction. We wait until there's a hole in the ozone layer before we stop the production of fluorocarbons. And many companies are waiting for the perfect security technology before making a serious investment.

There is no better time than the present to begin developing an appropriate enterprise security architecture. If you wait until you're business is compromised, you've waited too long. Chances are your Web site has already been assaulted.

Yes, holes in the ozone and rising average temperatures do have a way of stirring us into action. For their part, DoS attacks spotlight a common Web vulnerability. By using tools readily available—for free—at a variety of "underground" Web sites, a hacker could stage a coordinated DoS attack on a Web site or Web sites of his or her choice. After a well-publicized attack, usually two things happen: The attackee does a serious review of its security mechanisms, and customers have their confidence shaken.

**After a well-publicized attack, usually two things happen: The attackee does a serious review of its security mechanisms, and customers have their confidence shaken.**

What we're suggesting is that it pays to invest in an appropriate security architecture. By that we mean it can often generate more revenue than it costs. But you must do your homework first, before plunking down cash for some firewall or encryption scheme. No self-respecting IT chief would suggest buying IT hardware and software before doing a thorough system analysis. Yet, companies often buy security systems before they've done a credible job of vulnerability testing.

## TAKING A HOLISTIC APPROACH

In the chapters that follow, we will look at a process for defining an enterprise security architecture, then examine the steps required to implement it. We will also show the critical interrelationship between objectives, organization, procedures, and technologies. The best intrusion alarm system is useless if it is not properly armed, and the best security approach won't work if people fail to do their part.

Today's security systems tend to focus on prevention, but that addresses only one-third of the need. Prevention creates a deterrent, but intrusions will occur. Now there is a growing interest in detection technologies, but again, they address one-third of the need. Once intrusion has taken place and been detected, a security environment must also support *response*. Without detection and response components, a prevention-only scheme is destined to fail. Even worse, if people believe the prevention mechanisms are perfect, they won't be looking for evidence of intrusion.

> **Today's security systems tend to focus on prevention, but that addresses only one-third of the need.**

Finally, we believe that too much focus has been centered on the Internet itself. Certainly, the Net enables people to tamper with Web sites half a world away. But the truth is, a lot of attacks are inside jobs. An appropriate security environment will provide a balance of security that operates both outside and inside the enterprise network. A lot of secrets are given up innocently through so-called social engineering methods. A private key algorithm may be very difficult to break, but that becomes moot if the holder is tricked into divulging it.

It was once said that IBM would invent a competitor where none apparently existed. The idea was to avoid complacency. With regard to security, though, there's no need to invent a threat. It may not seem imminent, but it's there.

# PART II

# The Benefits

# CHAPTER 3

# A Business Enabler

Security measures taken as a response to threats and vulnerabilities are important, and we will certainly address those approaches. But there's another side to security that is often given short shrift. Whereas every business needs some level of security, some businesses are not possible without it.

For example, let's say your company would like to sell information content on the Web. It would also like to protect the intellectual property rights of the creators of that content. In the first instance, you need a way to distribute paid-for content. In the second, you need a way to prevent unauthorized duplication and distribution of that paid-for content. Can you do it? If you can, you've enabled an e-book business, and security is a key enabler.

You are a large automobile manufacturer faced with cutting waste out of the design-to-production cycle, and shortening your time to market. Why not create an environment for manufacturers and suppliers that speeds up everyone's ability to respond? All of them would share the same network infrastructure, but private transactions would remain private. Can intellectual property and bid transaction privacy be preserved? If so, you've enabled a new automotive industry exchange, and security is a key enabler.

A major credit-card company sees a growing opportunity in e-commerce transactions. It also sees a competitive advantage if it can achieve "card present" levels of risk and fees for online credit card purchases. Is it possible? If practical, it enables a payment mechanism that can lower merchant costs significantly, and security is a key enabler.

Will real estate sales, including title transfers, ever be done completely online? What about car sales and title transfers? Will we ever be able to vote online without substantial risk of fraud?

All of the above are instances in which appropriate security is a key enabler; it is part and parcel of the rest of the value proposition. The key point here is that, when security-based risk is evaluated and integrated into other business-related risks, the end result may be a model that produces more revenue than it could without that security component. And if the incremental revenues are higher than the cost of that security component, then the latter has literally paid for itself.

> **When security-based risk is evaluated and integrated into other business-related risks, the end result may be a model that produces more revenue than it could without that security component.**

## ENABLING NEW BUSINESS EXTENSIONS: THE E-BOOK BUSINESS

In the publishing business, authors trust that their publishers will protect their intellectual property. In the music business, artists have the same expectations of their production and distribution companies.

We've seen the music industry take off its gloves when the Napster Web site began facilitating the exchange of digitized music among its membership. The issue concerned copyright infringement and how to digitally distribute music while fairly compensating artists.

So, what about books? If a publisher offers an e-book (a digitized book), what protections are there to cover the author's intellectual property? We asked Richard Sarnoff, president of Random House New Media and Corporate Development, which includes Random Ventures, Random House's investment company. One of their investments is Xlibris—an online publisher and distributor of paper and e-books.

"First of all, there are major differences between music and books," said Sarnoff. "Virtually all music consumers already have a collection of unprotected digital music files (i.e., CDs) in their homes. The same is not true for books. Therefore, music lends itself to 'file trading,' while books do not. Another difference is that music is already sampled a great deal (via radio). The same is not true for books. And while MP3 compression is not as resolute as raw CD sound, listeners do not seem to care. Readers, on the other hand, prefer to read from paper rather than screens today. And, finally, there are significant age demographic differences between music and book consumers. The latter spans a huge spectrum compared with the former," Sarnoff explained.

In visiting the Xlibris Web site, we found an opportunity to purchase paper or e-book versions. The e-book versions are paid for and downloaded, then viewed using an Adobe Acrobat utility. You can read the book on your computer, but you cannot copy or print it out. Of course, you could do a screen capture, page-by-page, and copy and print it that way, but it would take longer than copying a physical book, page-by-page, on a copier machine.

"What we've done is make it far easier to purchase an e-book than it is to pirate one. The goal is to establish legal, positive consumer behavior at the very earliest stages," Sarnoff pointed out. "The outcome, of course, is still in question. I believe that ultimately people will gravitate toward one type of e-reading device, but I'm unwilling to bet on whether it will be more palmtop- or laptop-like. Once we know what that reading device will be, we can take further steps toward protecting the copyrights," he concluded.

> **"What we've done is make it far easier to purchase an e-book than it is to pirate one. The goal is to establish legal, positive consumer behavior at the very earliest stages," says Richard Sarnoff, president of Random House New Media.**

In essence, though, Xlibris is creating a new business application. It is able to reduce book production costs and pass some of that savings along to consumers, while providing authors with their royalties and providing appropriate security for copyright protection. At the same time, Xlibris changes the business for traditional publishing. Authors of books that would attract limited audiences now have an alternative to self-publishing. For example, it would require a smaller number of book purchasers to recoup the e-book production investment than it would for a hardbound or soft-cover book. As a result, Xlibris can support a broader selection of topics and lesser-known authors without putting its profitability at risk.

## ENABLING TOTALLY NEW BUSINESS MODELS: THE EXCHANGE BUSINESS

The Internet exchange business has the power to radically change the relationships among manufacturers and suppliers. While security isn't the primary success factor, it is certainly one of the top three.

At its core, an exchange is a collection of buyers and sellers—not all that different from an online auction. But the similarities end there. In this case, the buyers are not simply browsing the sellers' stalls looking for an already existing item; they are telling the sellers exactly what they need, and then looking for competitive offers from interested sellers. At the same time, the exchange has an opportunity to provide industry-oriented news, classified ads, and the like. In addition, the exchange can provide the payment services needed to cement various deals.

To be sure, every industry already has manufacturer–supplier relationships in place, and pre-Web mechanisms for working together. The Web, however, provides a way of speeding up the whole process, making it more open and competitive, and lowering costs. For example, Covisint, the automobile industry exchange founded by DaimlerChrysler, Ford, and General Motors, is being touted as a way of shaving as much as $3,000 off the price of a new car. What's more, it is seen as a way of shortening the new-car development cycle by nearly half.

An industry exchange is no simple matter. The benefits, of course, are its inclusive aspects. By enabling more manufacturers and suppliers to engage each other in a common environment, both sides enjoy a more open and competitive milieu. On the other hand, each participant has intellectual property and trade secret information, and expects it to be handled with appropriate levels of security.

Those who manage an exchange have to guard against both information security risk and the possibility of collusion. The former is a people, process, and technology issue; the latter is primarily a people and process issue. So, let's see how Covisint deals with each one.

## Covisint

At first, there was talk around the automobile industry of a GM exchange, a Ford exchange, and a Chrysler exchange.

Each original equipment manufacturer (or OEM) would set up its own networked exchange with its suppliers as a means of streamlining the request-for-quotes (RFQ) and bid processes.

When the suppliers got wind of it, they said, "No way." Why? Because it meant they would be dealing, typically, with two or three different exchanges and all the duplication of effort that implied. Each OEM had just one exchange to worry about. So, when the OEMs relented and discussed creating a single exchange to be shared among them and their suppliers, the suppliers were initially elated.

Bowing to pressure from their suppliers, the Big Three automobile makers then began talking about a joint exchange, and Covisint was born. While gestating, the embryonic exchange was managed by a team of three, one manager each from the founding companies. Peter Weiss, from DaimlerChrysler, felt the security risks were actually mitigated by the exchange.

"Compare it to what goes on now," said Weiss. "How secure is it to send a diagram over a fax machine? There are suppliers already handling ten different projects for five different OEMs. They have their internal security mechanisms in place, and Covisint will only serve to add security to the overall environment." Nevertheless, Weiss agreed, security had to be a given in order for Covisint to proceed from concept to prototype.

But it wasn't information security, per se, that caught the attention of the Federal Trade Commission (FTC). It was the possibilities for antitrust behavior. They were worried about the OEMs using their collective power to push supplier prices artificially lower. So, just when it looked like things were starting to roll, the FTC began an official inquiry into Covisint's emerging practice decisions.

"We had to have very detailed business plans in order to answer questions about antitrust. Plus, we had to make governing procedures and to dig deep to understand right away how we were going to operate," Weiss explained.

To complicate things even more, because of Chrysler's merger with Daimler-Benz, the exchange would also need the blessing of Germany's FTC counterpart, the Bundeskartellamt.

Covisint understood that to enable its exchange it had to convince its participants that their information was secure, and to convince the suppliers and government agencies that it included processes in its security architecture to deal with antitrust behavior. In fact, there are now assurance programs in place that deal with neutrality issues for exchanges such as Covisint. After a neutrality audit, such exchanges can receive a seal attesting to their compliance. A neutrality seal certifies that the exchange has satisfied a strict list of criteria and gives users a strong measure of comfort that it is acting in a totally neutral, unbiased fashion.

> **A neutrality seal certifies that the exchange has satisfied a strict list of criteria and gives users a strong measure of comfort that it is acting in a totally neutral, unbiased fashion.**

"In our case," said Weiss, "we reacted sharply and put in bylines that OEMs cannot aggregate together—period. We agreed there will be no aggregate buying. An OEM is free to deal with its own supply chain, as before, and that's all."

Evidently it was enough, because when all the poking and probing was done by the U.S. and German government trade investigators, Covisint was given a conditional green light. We say "conditional" because the FTC has reserved the right to reexamine the exchange and its operations once it is up and running.

Now, with the initial approval of the FTC and Bundeskartellamt, Covisint's wheels started to turn in earnest. "By year's end we were doing over $400 million worth of auction transactions," Weiss disclosed. "And we're now at $500 million worth in auctions and catalog transactions."

In retrospect, Covisint was a response to a business rather than a security need. An exchange could grease the wheels of automobile design and development while lowering the costs by eliminating lots of the waste. But information security, transaction privacy, and antitrust sensitivity were cornerstones to its acceptance. The key was to deliver the supply chain transforming ele-

> An exchange could grease the wheels of automobile design and development while lowering the costs by eliminating lots of the waste. But information security, transaction privacy, and antitrust sensitivity were cornerstones to its acceptance.

ments without compromising any of the security expectations that now exist among OEMs and their suppliers.

An important factor in Covisint's operation is the information backbone provided by Advanced Network Exchange (ANX), which has a track record in global integration of advanced, high-performance networking. This gives Covisint a security advantage. "IPSEC (a standard that supports authentication and encryption) is one element of ANX's overall security policy," said Peter Rosamilia, chief strategy officer for ANXeBusiness Corp. "Another is our rigor in service provider selection, plus features in the network aimed specifically at security and the members-only model for ANX access," Rosamilia explained.

Both Weiss and Rosamilia agreed that the security challenge, going forward, would be integrating the supply chain element of Covisint. There is a multitiered aspect to the supply chain such that a direct supplier to GM, for example, has its own upstream suppliers who each, in turn, have their own suppliers. Any real breakthrough in overall speed will rest on the ability to integrate as many of the supply tiers as possible into the mix, and to do so while preserving information security and privacy transactions. Then, too, Covisint and ANX face the security issues alluded to in Chapter 2 by EDS's Milholland. With a multitiered supply chain integrated into the whole, each new supplier poses an unknown security risk to the overall exchange.

Said Rosamilia, "I think trying to collapse the multitiered supply chain and giving them access to information normally held at OEM level is one crucial element of the challenge, and the other is bringing technology solutions to suppliers who have not earlier made such investments."

## Enabling a Collection of Exchanges

Security is not only an enabler for an industry exchange such as Covisint; it can be an enabler of a collection of exchanges. Take VerticalNet, for example. VerticalNet is essentially two things: a managed collection of exchanges, and a provider of tools for creating exchanges.

Mark Walsh, VerticalNet's chairman, said this about his customers' security expectations: "It maps against their size. The smaller customers are less concerned about security, the medium ones are more concerned, and the largest are paranoid. At the end of the day, the biggest companies have the most to lose, so they're the most concerned. For example, if a large company's purchasing and sales information got into the hands of a competitor, that company would be irreparably harmed. So, they're paranoid." In effect, then, VerticalNet's security architecture—its people, processes and technologies—must keep the exchanges separated so that each appears to be the only exchange in action.

Says Walsh, "There's another aspect to our business that security enables. On the B2B auction side, anonymity is king. Though there are many companies engaged in transactions, each transaction is one-on-one and totally private. It has to be, and we make sure it is, by modeling our security after that of world-class financial services systems. In fact, we have an advantage over the financial services folks in that our employees have no vested interest in the transaction. We're not brokers; we're facilitators."

The digital age is full of creative possibilities like the ones outlined here, each made possible by fertile imaginations and powerful security.

# CHAPTER 4

# It's All about Trust

One could argue that all businesses are about trust, but banking epitomizes the statement. Think about it: We give banks our money and trust that they'll keep it safe. They lend our money and we trust that they'll use due diligence before handing over the cash. They use our money to redeem our checks, and we trust they'll use appropriate caution in authorizing those payments. A branch may be robbed or burned down or destroyed in an earthquake, but we trust that they have managed those risks and that their insurance will keep us whole.

Security is clearly a key part of a bank's value proposition. The trust we have in banks is earned by their security consciousness. That massive vault door that protects the safe deposit boxes and their contents speaks volumes about security. So do those double-key-locked boxes that hold our deeds, stocks, and important papers.

Some of that earned trust made the transition to automatic teller machines (ATMs). Initially, most people approached ATMs with caution. They trusted the ATM's (and the bank's) ability to give out cash, but many were less willing to make deposits that way, at first. The fact that the ATM was physically attached to the bank added to the sense of trust. As this mode of banking became more familiar, the trust grew, and ATMs became more popular.

Online banking is in its relative infancy. Coupled with its network dependencies, it tends to be subject to knee-jerk reactions to online incidents. So, for example, when Web commerce takes a hit following a well-publicized attack, online banking also sees a temporary drop in activity. And that's what makes the Web both so interesting and so perplexing. When a bank branch is robbed, people do not stop banking or shopping in its neighborhood. When an ATM is vandalized, people do not stop using ATMs. However, when something criminal happens to one Web site, the whole network and all its Web sites are tarred with the same brush.

**When something criminal happens to one Web site, the whole network and all its Web sites get tarred with the same brush.**

Think about it, though. No bank president has ever said, "It's impossible for anyone to rob this branch." Instead, they imply, "Don't worry about robberies; if they happen, we've got you covered." And we don't worry. Yet somehow, people expect the network neighborhood to be absolutely safe, and when bad things happen, they lose faith (albeit temporarily). Does it have to be this way? We don't think so, and neither does Bank of America.

Rhonda MacLean, senior vice president and director of information protection at Bank of America, is one of what she considers a new generation of security professionals. "A lot of the original pros came out of law enforcement or government, and they're great at what they do. But few of them could elevate the security discussion to a business-level discussion," she explained. "And that's what's necessary."

MacLean concurs with our view of security as an enabler. "It's all about meeting our customers' expectations, their confidence and their trust." She sees the technology aspect of security as just that—one aspect. "It takes three components—people, process, and technology—and the end result should be preservation of trust.

"Historically, customers did most of their banking at the local branch, but banking at the branch was not always the most convenient. Operationally, ATMs offered the customer flexible service hours and location convenience. There was an adaptation period during which customers grew more confident and trusting in transacting through ATMs."

Online banking offers even more convenience and flexibility to the customer. However, just as with ATMs, the banks will have to help customers realize the same confidence and trust in online banking that they experience in branch banking.

"To be sure, publicized incidents of Internet crimes have a negative impact on all kinds of Web transactions, including online banking. But I believe over time people will gain a more realistic perspective about online banking risks, and the confidence and trust they now have with in-branch and ATM banking will expand to embrace online banking, too."

MacLean prefers to talk about trust rather than security. "Trust is at the heart of what is being delivered through good security practices. I can't say no one will ever penetrate our security, just as I can't say no one will ever rob a Bank of America branch," she reasons. "But I can say that if someone does rob one of our branches, you can trust that you'll be protected. That's how I see security, as an enabler of expanded online banking trust."

> **"The reason they put brakes on a car is so that you can go fast. Security is the brake that will enable online and e-commerce banking to go fast," says Rhonda MacLean, SVP and director of information protection, Bank of America.**

To MacLean, an investment in security is an investment in speeding up and growing the adoption of online banking and e-commerce services. "The reason they put brakes on a car is so that you can go fast," she quips. "Security is the brake that will enable online and e-commerce banking to go fast."

We would add, though, that banks have the power to speed up the adoption of online banking, and it has to do with managing perceptions. When people walk into a bank, they see that vault door, those rugged safe deposit boxes, the security cameras, and the rest. But a Web site is a set of screen images to the Internet user. There is really no hint of the people, processes, and technologies that underlie it.

People need a sense of safety if they are to grow more trusting. And that safety need not be absolute; in fact, it can't be. Banks just have to demonstrate that, like the bricks-and-mortar bank on the corner, the online version is security conscious and will protect our money and our information. We believe that the banks that do the best job of getting that message across will have first-mover advantages in the online banking share of mind.

## TRUST AND CREDIT CARDS

Another business that relies on trust and security is the credit card industry. Consider VISA or Master Card. The security environment is meant to protect the card issuers, the merchants, and the consumers. Most consumers know, for example, that their liability limit for fraudulent use of their cards is $50. Merchants know that their transaction costs are different when a purchaser hands them a credit card than when they get the card information over the phone or Internet. This reflects the increased risk of such transactions to both the card issuer and the merchant.

Without question, VISA and Master Card thought about the effect on credit card use of making the liability limit lower or higher than its current $50, and they picked that limit because of several factors. For one, most consumers would be willing to bear that risk for the convenience of credit card purchasing. For another, if fraud did occur, the $50 would offset the cost to the issuer. A higher limit would have increased the offset cost but decreased card use, along with fee and interest revenues. A lower limit might have increased the issuers' exposure without increasing card use and commensurate revenues. The goal was to pick an optimal limit—one that optimized consumers' sense of usage safety and limited exposure, and at the same time optimized the issuers' revenues, managing the risk by offsetting exposure with increased card-use revenues.

The rest of the security environment is designed to make that $50 limit an optimal figure. Every new card that is issued requires the recipient to call in and authenticate it. The cards are useless before that. When cardholders call in, they are asked for information that is not part of the card delivery package. Sometimes, simply verifying that the telephone number used to call in is the same as that in the card issuer's records is sufficient. The other key aspect is that every card has an expiration date. So, even if it were to fall into the wrong hands, its use is automatically time-limited.

Bolstering this security environment are the real-time authentication systems that merchants now use. If a card is lost or stolen, the issuer can cancel that card number within minutes of receiving notification. Individual issuers have also employed systems that examine card transactions looking for anomalous behavior. It is not uncommon for card users to be contacted by such issuers to verify that they've made specific purchases. All of these changes have mitigated the issuers' and merchants' risks substantially, and consumers seem content with the $50 liability limit. The net effect is that security is a key aspect of the bankcard credit delivery service, and its cost and effectiveness have been cranked into the overall business process.

## SOMETHING OLD, SOMETHING NEW: USING SECURITY TO COMPETITIVE ADVANTAGE

Before there was a commercial Internet, there were private networks. Companies leased private lines and paid lots of money for the convenience of networking and the assurance of privacy. With the opportunity to send encrypted information over the public Internet infrastructure, companies thought they had the best of both worlds—the convenience and privacy of the private networks and the low costs of Internet networking. Thus was born the concept of virtual private networks, or VPNs.

But VPNs, like everything else attached to the Internet, are vulnerable. In fact, Bruce Schneier, author of *Secrets and Lies*, calls them a "hole through your firewall." Companies unwilling to risk outsourcing their essential IT applications infrastructure had little alternative until Qwest Cyber.Solutions (QCS) came along.

For customers running complex business applications such as Oracle, SAP, and Siebel, QCS removes the public-network risks with delivery over Qwest's global infrastructure. "We have a homogenous IP network—end-to-end— and we own it," explained John Charters, the company's president and CEO. Like a private information road parallel to a public information highway, QCS's network is for customers only, but it allows the same kinds of vehicles to travel across it—IP packets. That means it takes no special systems or software to use it, other than those already used for any other TCP/IP-compliant network (read "Internet").

QCS uses its private networking infrastructure to enable and support its applications service provider (ASP) business. An ASP contracts with a company to provide and support applications, such as enterprise resource planning (ERP) or customer relationship management (CRM). The services are provided over the network, and the ASP is responsible for the maintenance, service, and upgrading of these large software systems.

Charters believes that ASP solutions hosted in Qwest's CyberCenters and delivered over the IP network provide added trust and credibility for customers that may be concerned about the potential vulnerability of the public Internet. "Remember, we're dealing with accounts payable, accounts receivable, client-list data, and other sensitive information. If that data got into the wrong hands, it would be harmful in many, many ways." It would also potentially expose Qwest Cyber.Solutions to legal redress by the companies involved.

While the homogenous network provides a solid foundation for security of business-critical application data, it is only the first weapon in Qwest Cyber.Solutions' arsenal. Focused on the flight to quality, QCS is developing the next layer of security as well. "We'll know proactively if someone is trying to hack our system," Charters claims. "We'll have extensive perimeter safeguards, plus intrusion detection systems, plus the policies and procedures that tie everything together."

In other words, though the global network is private, QCS leaves virtually nothing to chance. QCS's use of VPN technology complements the inherent security of the IP network and even further reduces security risk. Finally, ASP customers need not fear any possible exposure of QCS's Web site, because they are two separate entities that are appropriately insulated from one another; therefore, ASP services would not be affected by this minimal risk, according to Charters.

## ENABLING GROWTH BY PROTECTING ONE'S ASSETS

We've talked about security as a business enabler in terms of its ability to enhance customer trust, value, and loyalty. And we've talked about how security itself has been the foundation of brand new business models and applications. What we haven't addressed yet is the notion of security as a form of enlightened self-interest. In other words, proactively embracing security is a means of warding off the three dreaded *L*s of the digital age: liability, lawsuits, and losses.

**Security is a form of enlightened self-interest. It's a means of warding off the three dreaded *L*s of the digital age: liability, lawsuits, and losses.**

We know that lawyers and insurers are drooling over what they see as the certain prospect of shareholder and other lawsuits stemming from, well, take your pick: a major system outage resulting in loss of Web access for a number of hours or days (think online trading); or negligence for not adequately protecting your systems against known vulnerabilities (by putting up some simple patches or using available tools to defend against DDoS attacks); or unwittingly allowing your company's or your employees' computers to serve as zombies for a concerted DDoS attack on another company.

Already, we're beginning to see a rise in new insurance products to address some of these factors. It is incumbent on all companies to whisk their current insurance policies and business continuity plans out of the file closet to determine whether the language and contingencies within adequately cover this new range of risks. And this can be tricky.

Basic property insurance provides coverage for damage to your business property, including, as a common example, damage due to weather-related incidents. Typically, those plans cover physical loss and damage to property. Does that mean you're covered for computer system losses? If winter rains cause your roof to leak on top of your servers, knocking them out, then sure, you're covered. But in situations

> **If winter rains cause your roof to leak on top of your servers, knocking them out, then sure, you're covered. But in situations that involve viruses, hacking damage, and the like, insurance companies may fight any claim attempts.**

that involve viruses, hacking damage, and the like, insurance companies may fight any claim attempts.

Even policies that include electronic data processing (EDP) endorsements (broad-brush and, therefore, often vague clauses that seeks to cover some electronic assets) don't always give you the coverage you think you're getting.

Even if you have good business continuity coverage, trying to put a value on a loss can be difficult. If your business deals heavily in electronic commerce or relies heavily on a networked supply chain, and your systems go down for a few days or even a week, the potential loss to your business can, we know, be huge. But if you're a B2B company, providing service to businesses rather than consumers, it can be much harder to put a figure on the loss. The same is true if you're already showing an operating loss. Thinking about these issues ahead of time; observing good security hygiene, such as putting in readily available patches; and reviewing your policies with in-house counsel can save you a lot of grief, annoyance, and cold hard cash in the long run.

## CONCLUSION: TRUST AND SECURITY

Security is a means to an end, and that end is trust. Where trust is a critical part of the value proposition—as in banking—security becomes a critical enabling factor. But the need for trust goes far beyond banking. We trust that companies we

**Security is a means to an end, and that end is trust.**

invest in will take appropriate steps to limit their exposure to all kinds of business risk, to protect stockholder interests. Information risk is a business risk. We trust that the companies we do business with will honor the confidential nature of our relationships, and have appropriate safeguards in place to protect our intellectual property and other trade secrets. People, processes, and technologies are all part of the trust equation.

# PART III

# The Approach

......................................................................

# CHAPTER 5

# A Multifaceted Process

"*Security is about culture and values. Senior management must take security as an issue of corporate governance, not as an issue of technology. It requires leadership, not technology. If your people are thinking right, they will identify and address security problems. If they view security as a nuisance and an impediment, they will work around it and subvert it.*"

William Malik, VP and Research Area Director, Gartner Group, December 28, 2000

During our interview with William Malik, we believe he hit the nail squarely on the head. Security is more about culture and values than about firewalls and intrusion detection systems. When he said, "If they view security as a nuisance ... ," he chose his words carefully. It isn't important what your security solution actually entails; what matters is how your people view it. That, in turn, suggests leadership and education first, so that subsequent decisions and policies are embraced rather than resisted.

This concept also suggests that processes and technology need to be tailored to both the business requirements and the corporate culture. Like a car alarm system, your security processes and technology won't work if someone forgets to arm them. And, even if they do work, like a car alarm,they may be ineffective because the warning is ignored. The ineffectiveness of car alarms has more to do with culture than technology.

Said Gartner's William Malik, "For security, the largest returns are in awareness. This means values, culture, and appropriate behavior. History is replete with examples of good management overcoming limitations of technology. On the other hand, we have no examples of good technology overcoming poor management."

> "For security, the largest returns are in awareness. This means values, culture, and appropriate behavior," said William Malik, vice president of the Gartner Group.

## THE PEOPLE PART OF THE PROCESS

People are your greatest security asset—and your biggest vulnerability. Kevin Mitnick, the infamous hacker, admitted he rarely had to resort to technical exploits.

We hear a lot about crackers (hackers with bad intent) tying up Web sites, nabbing credit card files, and defacing Web site home pages. Here are some cases, taken from old copies of *Computer Security Alert*, that you've probably never heard about. In both cases, the perpetrators depended on social engineering, on getting someone to give away the store.

## No Networks Involved

A small engineering firm was betting the farm on its unique new product. Everyone had been working long hours for more than a year getting it ready for market. All indications were that its closest competitor was at least a year away from bringing a similar concept to market. So, the president took a hard-earned vacation. A day or two later, in waltzed a well-dressed man carrying an expensive attaché case and sporting a Rolex watch. He explained that he was consulting for the president, handed out several business cards, and proceeded to "schmooze" with some of the other executives and managers.

No one questioned his credentials. In fact, they set him up in a conference room, gave him a tour of the R&D area, and introduced him to engineering. When he left that area, he asked for and was given a copy of the new product block diagrams and schematics. "I do a lot of work at home," he explained to them.

Later he took a bunch of people out to lunch and queried the finance people about costs and suppliers, and the marketing people about product launch plans and schedules. At six o'clock that night, he left. No one ever saw him again. But the competitor launched a remarkably similar product one month before the original company did, inflicting heavy marketing damage. That was a case of social engineering. The criminal got what he wanted in person, rather than by machine.

## Take My PIN Codes, Please

In another case, an expert on computer security was explaining to an audience how easy it was to get people to give up the "goods." Noting looks of incredulity in the audience, he picked up a cell phone that was amplified so that all could eavesdrop. He punched in 411 and asked for a well-known bank's telephone number. Then he called and got himself transferred to its computer help desk. "Hi," he began, "who's supervising tonight?" He was told it was Laura, and asked to be connected.

"Hey, Laura," he said, "looks like you've got problems." She asked him what he meant. He told her all her systems were down. "They're fine," she argued, "everything looks okay."

Well, he told her, his monitors showed that everything was down. "Sign off," he told her, and the audience could hear the key clicks. "Now, sign on again," he ordered, and more key clicks were audible. "Nothing," he muttered. He asked her to sign off once more, and she did. Then he said, "Laura, I'm going to sign on as you to see what's going on. I need your user ID and password." And she gave them to him.

"Nope," he said a few seconds later, "that didn't do it." Then he said, "I know what's wrong. You're looking at the day-old cache. You think you're online but you're not. So, log on, again." She did. "I'll verify it, now, by comparing PIN codes. Your list should be different from the current list. Just give me the first five or so." And Laura began reading off those PIN codes.

What is so interesting about both of these cases is that in other companies, many employees would probably have acted the same way. In the absence of hard-and-fast rules and procedures, we're more inclined to give people the benefit of the doubt. And that's exactly what "social engineers" count on.

## TURNING THOSE VULNERABILITIES INTO ASSETS

Turning your biggest vulnerability into your greatest asset requires no draconian measures. You don't have to fire everyone and start over. What you have to do is make people part of the solution.

Like everything else about security, this too is a process, and the process starts at the top of the organization. The security objectives driven by business priorities have got to be framed into a comprehensive set of security practices. These have to be developed in concert with company executives, business units, human resources, information technology, and security groups within the company.

Like a good marketing campaign, the security campaign needs to be rolled out, accompanied by well-crafted materials and training programs. It needs to be integrated into human resource standard procedures

**Like a good marketing campaign, the security campaign needs to be rolled out, accompanied by well-crafted materials and training programs.**

and made part of both the orientation and on-going training curricula.

If we had to make a choice between a well-briefed and well-trained staff using barely adequate technologies, or a staff equipped with the latest and most up-to-date technologies but lacking comprehensive policies and training, we would choose the former. But our ideal choice would be a well-briefed and well-trained staff equipped with the most effective technologies.

The Gartner Group's Malik commented, "Imagine an employee walking down the hall who happens to see someone doing something that might be wrong. Now, ask three questions. Would he know if what he saw was wrong or not? Would he choose to report it? If he were to pick up the phone, would he know whom to call? In other words, does the organization have a basic awareness of security and appropriate use, does the organization have a culture that supports security, and finally does the organization have the management mechanisms to reinforce that culture? If the answers are 'yes,' 'yes,' and 'yes,' you've won. If not, there are basic problems—which technology will not solve."

## Making Your People Part of the Solution

The human part in any security solution is primary. Both Henry Teng, the former chief of information security at eBay, and Howard Schmidt, Microsoft's chief security officer, relied on people more than on technologies when it came to identifying an exception event.

"You need to detect that you're under attack. That means knowing your network's characteristics through constant monitoring. If you see the same flood of traffic at 1 a.m. as you normally see at 7 p.m. and you know your network traffic patterns, then your Web site is probably under attack, but it takes a group of people to confirm that determination," Teng explained. After the DDoS attacks in February 2000, eBay and Yahoo! made significant changes in how they detect and respond to such attacks. "The strategy isn't to completely prevent them. In fact, you cannot. The strategy is to handle them appropriately so that what formerly resulted in hours of disruption can now be contained in minutes," said Teng.

We asked Schmidt to give us a brief description of a more recent incident in which an intruder gained access to Microsoft's network. "I was made aware the minute it escalated from a help-desk function. As part of the process when something looks out of line they escalate to Security. That's what they were trained to do, and that's what they did. If they hadn't reacted as quickly, the incident could easily have grown in scale," Schmidt stated. "At the time, I was getting ready to leave for Germany to participate in the G8 Cyber Crime Summit in Berlin. My group said, 'We're seeing something strange.' And I told them to keep me totally informed and start tracking the suspicious activity," Schmidt recalled.

According to Schmidt, the system worked. He never believed that the network could not be penetrated. "I'm realistic about it. It happens and you have to deal with it. We detected the intrusion and followed all the procedures. We found that hole and eliminated it," he stated. As for changes to the security environment in the wake of the intrusion, Schmidt said they were very minor. "Ours is a Windows 2000 environment, and we use the security tools built into that operating system. And that's key. With a process in place that enables you to detect and respond, as well as prevent the great majority of intrusion attempts, you have all the pieces. But you have to act on it. If you use those tools on a periodic basis, it won't help you respond appropriately. You must identify the intrusion as early as possible if you're going to squelch it, track it, and mitigate any damage," he advises.

> **You must identify the intrusion as early as possible if you're going to squelch it, track it, and mitigate any damage," says Howard Schmidt, chief security officer for Microsoft.**

## LOOKING BEYOND YOUR ENTERPRISE

An appropriate security environment has to account for both your company's network and others associated with it. An "insider" at a partner company may seem like an "outsider" at your company, but if your networks are linked, the distinctions disappear.

In this era of myriad mergers and acquisitions, the problem is compounded, and attention to system integration controls (SIC) is called for. Whether through merger, acquisition, or joint venture, your enterprise has changed. Whenever systems marry, some in-built controls come along for the ride. These inherited controls may be inadequate to your current operating environment. Similarly, many companies invest in powerful ERP (Enterprise Resource Planning) systems to improve efficiency and responsiveness. However, because the speed with which these new systems are implemented is often critical to profitability, designing and implementing effective controls and security are not always emphasized. Such an oversight can lead to inadequate process controls, high levels of security risk, and other process failures.

EDS's Milholland has to deal not only with his own company's security challenges, but those of many of his customers. The same was true when he was at Boeing earlier in his career. "What we realized at Boeing, as we acquired new companies, is we don't really know anything about their level of security. When we would bring company B into the fold, we had to wonder what's at the other end of its pipes," Milholland said.

"As we grew and expanded, that became one of our major worries. How much additional exposure have we added? This is both a cultural and a technical dilemma, and you can't assume anything. You have to work to ensure a consistent security environment as your company grows," he explained. "EDS is much the same—perhaps more so— because we grow by outsourcing other people's networks to us, and each one increases the overall nodal structure. We have to make sure our security practices are rolled through the new additions. It's a straightforward exercise, but it's difficult and detailed," he summed up.

What comes through very loud and clear is that a security environment must be multifaceted, and the organization's security vigilance must be steadfast and up-to-date. What's more, your environment extends beyond your enterprise. It includes every other enterprise whose network is associated with your own.

Is your security architecture accomplishing what you think it is? Don't rely upon your own company's ability to prevent, detect, and respond. You need some assurance.

## THE VALUE OF OUTSIDE VALIDATION

"Never be a prophet in your own land," advises Microsoft's Schmidt. "Get outside validation that your security environment is doing what you think it does."

Microsoft's approach involves divided responsibilities. The day-to-day surveillance, updates, patches, and activities are all internal functions and responsibilities. There's even another layer of internal people who serve as "the checkers of the checkers," said Schmidt.

But Microsoft periodically brings in outside help to verify the effectiveness of and identify current vulnerabilities in its security capabilities. "Of course, we have experience with our own security environment, and through our business we have a perspective on other environments too. But you can never have too much insight, so you need to choose an outside team that has complementary knowledge and experience, and let them rattle your doorknobs and windows, too," Schmidt recommends.

For its part, Exodus Communications also solicits outside verification. "It's sometimes surprising the kinds of things they'll find," says CEO Ellen Hancock. "We had a card-access data center with electronic locking doors and sensors. It turned out that you could trip the sensor by putting a piece of paper between the top of the door and the doorframe. It was something we'd never thought of trying. Of course, we replaced the sensors once they discovered that flaw."

## A NEVER-ENDING EFFORT

If there's one thing that all the executives we interviewed agreed upon, it's that most companies don't fully appreciate the life cycle aspect of security. Says EDS's Terry Milholland, "You've put processes and countermeasures in place and they age. You have to have an approach that is continually looking and updating." Part of that life cycle aspect is recognizing the benefits and pitfalls of changing technologies.

### New Technologies, New Challenges, New Trade-offs

As new technologies are created and adopted, they often provide new benefits while posing new challenges. Any security architecture aimed at long-term effectiveness has got to address the reality of technological progress and concomitant added risk.

As in life, there's a flip side to everything in technology. For example, TCP/IP's broadcast packet mode enables a user to send information to every node on the system. The intention is to make life easier for network users by giving them a way to send data to several others without having to list all their individual addresses. But that broadcast capability, in the hands of a "Smurfer" (a particular kind of DoS attacker), is a means of amplifying an attack.

The attacker simply sends an ICMP ECHO packet (a common system diagnostic procedure) broadcasted to a large network of computers. In response to the ECHO packet, every computer on the network that receives it will respond with an ICMP ECHO_REPLY. Now, here's the catch: The original packet sent by the attacker has a phony source address on it (an action called "spoofing"). It is the address of the target of the attack. As a result, all those ECHO_REPLY packets come flooding into the target's Web site, either slowing things down or crashing the server in the process.

Encryption is another two-sided coin. If you send information in clear text and someone intercepts that information, they can read it. If you send information in encrypted form and someone intercepts it, the receiver has gibberish unless he or she also has the decryption key. So at first glance, it would seem to make sense to simply encrypt everything that enters a network or that is stored in a modestly secured location.

However, it takes a lot of computing power to encrypt and decrypt information. That's one of the reasons why every Internet transaction isn't done in the Secure Sockets Layer (SSL). It would take too much time and use too many computing resources. So when you go to an e-commerce site and you browse around looking for something to buy, all that data interaction is unencrypted. It's only when you're ready to buy the item that you are switched to SSL.

Here's another trade-off. When you choose a password on most sites, that password is encrypted and stored. That's good. Each time you enter that password, it is encrypted and compared against the encrypted password previously chosen and stored. That's also good. But if you forget your password, what happens? Generally, you have to create a new one. Why? Because that Web site probably cannot decrypt the encrypted password, either. So passwords provide good security, but managing them can be a pain.

## PKI—The Magic Bullet?

There are those who say a public key infrastructure, or PKI, is the answer to most critical security requirements. Simply put, PKI is an encryption/decryption technology that uses two keys—a public key and a private key. Information is encrypted using the public key, and decrypted using the private key. Should that private key be lost or corrupted, it may be impossible to decrypt the encrypted information. Remember those passwords?

Imagine an exploit in which the attacker somehow compromises a private key, creating a permanently encrypted document set. The information hasn't been stolen; it has simply been rendered unusable. The 1960s James Bond film,

*Goldfinger*, was about a plot to explode a tiny-yield nuclear bomb in the bowels of Fort Knox. The idea wasn't to steal the gold, but to simply make it unusable by making it all radioactive.

Now, encryption and decryption were not developed to make things unusable. They were intended to keep information unusable by those not authorized to receive it. Microsoft Outlook wasn't intended as a distribution vehicle for the Love Bug virus, either. How things were intended to be used, and how they may be used, are often two very different things.

### Keeping Current

If you are going to have appropriate security, you must keep pace with changes in technology and risk. We believe that is a given. But keeping current is a full-time job, in fact, several full-time jobs. There are myriad organizations and Web sites that play very useful roles in keeping us all informed. They run the gamut from CERT, a government-funded organization, to AntiOnline.com, whose tag line is, "Hackers know the weaknesses in your system; shouldn't you?"

> If you are going to have appropriate security, you must keep pace with changes in technology and risk.

In its earlier days, AntiOnline was part of the hacker underground, praising the latest exploits and extolling the virtues of hacker folk heroes. Today, though, the site offers news and information aimed at security professionals. And it gets lots of readership, judging from interspersed ads from companies like Microsoft and VeriSign.

Another source, The Privacy Foundation, first alerted the media about what is called the wiretapping flaw. When senders and recipients are using Microsoft Outlook, Outlook Express, or Netscape 6 Mail, a sender can insert a JavaScript code that alerts them when that message has been opened or forwarded, and will also capture any added text in the forwarded version.

The various surveys of network breaches and other security incidents all indicate that in a large majority of cases, the intrusion was accomplished by taking advantage of widely publicized weaknesses in popular operating systems or applications. In most cases, patches or other fixes for those weaknesses had been available well before the attack.

So the odds stack up like this: Even if your Web site is relatively inconspicuous, it will be scanned for vulnerabilities. If you are not diligent about taking first-order precautions (e.g., no null passwords—a setting whereby no password has been selected and anyone can gain access; no programs in default configurations; and the like), you will be targeted for intrusion. It's like parking your car in a seedy part of town with the doors unlocked and the key in the ignition.

Large company or small, your network and information security will be enhanced by keeping up with news about vulnerabilities in popular system components, and making changes that mitigate or eliminate those vulnerabilities.

Every new technology that comes along offers both new benefits and new risks. The move to wireless network access, for example, provides new conveniences and new vulnerabilities, just as the cellular telephone did 16 years ago.

## THINK "EVOLUTION," NOT "REVOLUTION"

We believe it is better to evolve than to revolt. History is replete with examples of people making revolutionary instead of evolutionary decisions. Sometimes that's good. Most of the time it leads to dead ends.

The ideal security architecture is one that meets your immediate needs and can grow to meet your future needs too. If we go back and explore some examples in other types of systems, we find that there were early indicators of how events would ultimately play out. You need to take advantage of those lessons.

For example, in the early days of local area networking, Ethernet and Token Ring competed fiercely for the major share of the market. It wasn't clear at that time which would ultimately prevail, as they both offered comparable performance and cost. Token Ring had the blessing of IBM, its inventor. Ethernet enjoyed the approval of Digital, Intel, and Xerox (its inventor). Slowly, the balance began to shift. More companies were building controller chips for Ethernet than for Token Ring. As a result, more OEMs were building Ethernet cards and writing Ethernet-compliant software. Economies of scale grew quickly and the cost of Ethernet solutions shifted downward much more quickly than was the case for Token Ring.

Later, Ethernet LANs became pervasive and Token Ring LANs edged closer and closer to the dustbin of history. But the need for more bandwidth and speed created an opportunity for faster LAN alternatives. The most prominent of these was a technology called Asynchronous Transfer Mode, or ATM. But it was a fundamentally different approach (think "revolutionary") to networking and was inherently incompatible with Ethernet.

As people explored the benefits and trade-offs, other people cobbled together ways to make Ethernet and ATM appear more compatible. Meanwhile, other companies looked at the investments already made in Ethernet-oriented media, systems, and software, and sought ways to make basic improvements in speed without changing the basic Ethernet structure (think "evolutionary"). This effort resulted in Fast Ethernet and Gigabit Ethernet—technology enhancements that permitted one to jump from 10 megabits per second to 100 megabits per second, then to 1 gigabit per second, all without having to replace Ethernet applications and media. Guess who won that battle?

The lesson for security solutions is to pick proven technologies that are designed for later expansion and scalability without requiring wholesale changes to their structures. As you will

**The lesson for security solutions is to pick proven technologies that are designed for later expansion and scalability.**

see, the success of anti-virus and intrusion detection systems rests on their ability to gather and maintain up-to-date libraries of viruses and exploit signatures. These are like fingerprints of known problem causers. No fingerprint, no match, no prevention. But gathering and maintaining that information is a major cost factor for those system vendors, so you need to assess their market shares, financial health, and long-term commitments. The right choice of system is a moving defense that can counter the moving threats. The wrong choice could easily become your company's Maginot Line.

# CHAPTER 6

# Prevention, Detection, and Response

"**R**eady. Fire. Aim." That's a common enough error in many aspects of business, and security is no exception. It assumes that you are ready, you have what you need, but you might not have applied it to the right target. Unfortunately, the real situation is usually more chaotic than that.

The diagram in Figure 6-1 (developed by Bank of America's Rhonda MacLean) captures the essence of an appropriate security environment: It's multifaceted. It involves people, processes, and technology. And it's driven by business needs.

## AN OUNCE OF PREVENTION ...

A lot of companies stop at "Ready" in their approach to computer security. They put a firewall between the enterprise network and the Internet, and assume they're ready. Bring on the hackers.

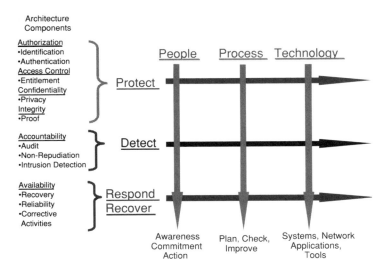

**figure 6-1    the comprehensive approach**

But firewalls are designed to let a lot of packets through. Okay, so you create a DMZ (demilitarized zone) using additional servers and firewalls. This is akin to building a moat around the castle. Does it make your system harder to penetrate? Sure. Does it make the system impossible to penetrate? No, especially when you consider the odds are about 80 percent that your attacker is in the castle, not on the other side of the moat.

## Use Strong Passwords

Often, the most effective penetration obstacles have nothing to do with your system software and firewall deployments. One way to gain an immediate increase in security is to make sure that everyone—administrators and users— employs difficult-to-crack passwords. That's it. This will provide an instant security boost whether you're using Windows NT, Unix, Linux or any other operating system.

The length of the password is the most important factor in its effectiveness. For example, a four-character password can typically be cracked in minutes. A seven-character password involves trillions of combinations and can take more than a month to crack.

You can further improve the anti-cracking strength of a password by using combinations of uppercase and lowercase characters, a mix of letters and numbers, and non-printing characters. Good passwords are like dead bolts. Doors with dead bolt locks can be smashed through, but no one gets in by slipping a credit card between the door and the jamb.

Other advancements include biometrics.

## Biometrics

Thumbprinting and iris recognition are two applications in an emerging field known as biometrics. Highly sensitive fingerpads or cameras can capture in a second information that proves that you are indeed you, more definitively than even a very strong password. These applications, though costly to implement, have the potential to save companies a considerable amount of money, not only because they eliminate a plethora of password issues (passwords can be lost, stolen, or corrupted), but because they place another obstacle in the path of insider security breaches.

The downside to this technology is that, if your digitized thumbprint were somehow stolen, there is no way of getting it back and certainly no way of replacing it. This is when attacks really get personal.

## Establish Clear and Enforceable Policies

Another immediate security improvement is gained by establishing, communicating, and enforcing stringent password policies. For example, it should be a serious infraction to leave a written password in the work area, or to divulge a password to anyone without explicit permission from a specific authority. Some companies do an excellent job of communicating and enforcing such policies. Within weeks of starting a job, for example, a new employee may receive a call from someone in IT asking for a password. A new employee who gives it up is reprimanded in no uncertain terms.

Similarly, rules need to be drafted, explained, and reinforced regarding system and network login and logoff. Optimal security is achieved when users log off whenever they leave a workstation, even for a minute or two. The user password is a key to a lock; when someone leaves a workstation after logging in, it's like leaving a checkout stand with the cash drawer open.

## Brick Up Those Backdoor Opportunities

Cracked passwords are used to come in through the front door. If you make that difficult enough, you're likely to dissuade a large number of potential intruders. What about other ways in? We've all seen movies in which determined bank robbers circumvent security systems by breaking into an adjoining building and tunneling through a wall or basement. That's just what determined intruders will try to do to your system. With the front door barred to them, they'll look for other ways in. Is your operating system in default configuration? Are there services made available outside your defensive perimeter that can be compromised, like file transfer protocol, or FTP?

Operating systems, fresh out of their shrink-wrap packaging, are ready to work—in default configuration. Think of them as millions of combination locks, all initially set up with the same combination. Once someone discovers that combination, he or she can open every lock that has not been configured beyond that original (default) setting. So change your combination by configuring the operating system, leaving nothing in "null password" mode.

Many services associated with Unix and Windows NT were included for completeness and convenience, but can be subverted for illicit purposes. One example is FTP, which permits the efficient downloading and uploading of large files. If you don't need a service, disable it. If you need it internally, prevent remote access to it. If you need it internally and externally, understand its vulnerabilities and install appropriate controls.

Internet servers have Internet Protocol (IP) addresses that are combinations of numeric characters and periods, like 205.174.17.54. To make it easier for users, though, more easily remembered addresses are associated with the servers, such as www.kpmg.com. When you click on that Web-site URL, a Domain Name Server (DNS) converts the mnemonic-oriented address into its physical IP address—the one with the numbers and periods. About 90 percent of all DNS's use the Berkeley Internet Name Domain, or BIND, software. In January 2001, the CERT Coordination Center at Carnegie Mellon University issued an alert, saying that "potentially devastating compromises" are probable unless that software is upgraded immediately. What's the problem? Earlier versions of BIND have a vulnerability that enables someone to shut down Web sites, reroute users to false sites, and intercept email access passwords and customer accounts.

The problem is potentially severe, and the cure is free, yet there's a good chance we will soon hear of exploits that take advantage of the problem. Invariably, popular software systems are shown to have vulnerabilities, and patches are created very quickly. But the responsibility for obtaining and installing those patches rests with people in your company. If they are diligent, know where to get current information about vulnerabilities, and respond quickly by installing patches or other fixes, then you're way ahead of the game. Is your company ahead ... or behind?

## If It's Really Top Secret, Keep It off the Net

Information that is really top secret should not be distributed over a network—encrypted or otherwise. Forget about all the estimates of how long it takes to decrypt this code or that code. During World War II, Germany felt very secure that its Enigma-encrypted transmissions could not be decrypted—but it was wrong. That mistake in judgment was largely responsible for Germany's inability to stop U.S. supply convoys from resupplying Britain.

If your information is sensitive, keep it locked up, and tightly control its physical distribution. Not doing so cost one company a billion dollars. According to Gartner Group's William Malik, the vice president and research area director responsible for information security strategies, a company whose contract bid information was accessible via its network was underbid by a competitor who got hold of

> **If your information is sensitive, keep it locked up, and tightly control its physical distribution. Not doing so cost one company a billion dollars.**

that bid information. The competitor won the contract, which was worth a billion dollars. Keep sensitive information in a safe.

As for your other data, rather than dividing it into hierarchical categories that correspond to specific policies, create just two categories—unsecured and secured. Unsecured information is that which can be readily distributed, without any sort of encryption or recipient authentication. Secured data should be backed up by whatever prevention, detection, and response solutions have been adopted, based on a thorough analysis of needs.

Here's how EDS's Terry Milholland sees it: "How valuable is your data? What's the cost of implementing the various levels of protection? Fully multilevel, secure operating systems do exist, but are very rigid. They don't allow people the flexibility to respond to changes in business, so they get dropped. Some companies employ two levels of security—confidential and limited. Sometimes, that is good enough."

By now it should be clear that prevention is at least equal parts technology and humanity. Are your business units, IT team, and security personnel all on the same page about potential problems and solutions? Do you have the tools you need? Do you have people who know how to use them? Are your employees doing their part by understanding their individual responsibilities and carrying them out? When you can answer "yes" to all these questions, you're "ready."

## DETECTION

You've done everything right, so far. You've aligned your security environment to business-driven exigencies. You've made sure the whole organization is involved in the solution. You've worked with experts to assess your penetration vulnerability and taken steps to eliminate or mitigate them. Everyone knows what his or her prevention role is, and everyone is acting responsibly.

That's great. You've reduced your intrusion probabilities—and your exposure—significantly. But they will never be reduced to zero. Can you reduce any of your business risks to zero? Therefore, someone will succeed in finding a way into your system. When they do, will you be able to tell?

First of all, realize that not every intrusion is discernible. If someone is using a legitimate ID and password to get in, that will not raise any flags unless the user tries to gain access to an area he or she is not authorized to enter. These intrusions are the hardest to detect, especially at the time of intrusion.

So, let's turn to a common physical security tool. When you walk into the lobby of a business headquarters, usually the first thing you see is a reception desk. The person or persons behind that desk greet you and ask you whom you are there to meet. They will ask you to sign a logbook, and they may enter your information directly into an automated system. Then, they will call the person you have come to see and verify that you are expected. In many cases, you will be issued a stick-on ID badge that identifies you as an escorted visitor. Usually, doors leading from the reception area to the business interior are electronically secured, so trying to run past the reception desk and into the building will not work.

The key part of this procedure is the logging process. The receptionists have captured your name, the date, the time, and your signature. Even if all that information is phony, they've captured an event—your visit. On the system side, you have many similar tools to work with.

The key part of this procedure is the logging process. The receptionists have captured your name, the date, the time, and your signature. Even if all that information is phony, they've captured an event—your visit. On the system side, you have many similar tools to work with.

## Taking Advantage of Built-In Logging Features

Operating systems typically come with integrated logging and auditing features that can be used to monitor activities involving critical resources. In addition, your network will provide services, such as Web servers, email servers, and databases, that include logging and auditing functions. These can be used to record activities related to those services. Such logs are essential in identifying intrusions, and can provide critical evidence later, for apprehending and prosecuting the intruder.

## Using Intrusion Detection Systems

Of the systems sold specifically for detecting intrusions, there are essentially two types—intrusion detection systems (IDS) and network intrusion detection systems (NIDS). Often, these are designed to work in conjunction with your network management consoles or platforms (such as HP's OpenView), whereby the IDS or NIDS alerts the console of an exception condition, and the console alerts an administrator, perhaps while simultaneously taking some programmed action.

The logging and auditing tools keep track of all transactions, legitimate and suspect. The IDS and NIDS look for suspect activities. An IDS is a host-based system that looks at high-level logging information provided to it by the operating system. It looks for suspicious patterns of activity on that single computer system. Thus, an IDS might be hosted on a DNS server, looking for attacks there.

In contrast, the NIDS is a perimeter-oriented device that examines streams of raw, or low-level, network traffic. A NIDS is used to identify attacks that involve low-level network manipulation, and to correlate attacks against multiple machines attached to the network.

These systems detect intrusions in several distinctly different ways. One way is through anomaly detection. That is, one type of IDS looks for exceptions to baseline operating conditions, such as CPU use, disk activity, user logins, file activity, and so on. The advantage to this method is that exceptions are detected without having to recognize specific attack characteristics.

With a NIDS, there are essentially two types of detection methodology. One is a signature analysis (e.g., a network grep technique) that sifts through raw packet data looking for particular patterns in network traffic. This is a pattern-matching technique. So, for example, it might be sifting through packets looking for a pattern such as */cgi-bin/phf*. This is a pattern associated with a familiar CGI script attack called "phf." This type of NIDS is checking packet "fingerprints," looking for a match with its database of existing "fingerprints." Its efficacy depends almost entirely on the current state of its database.

The other NIDS technique is called protocol analysis. It is designed to find all instances of an attack, not only those whose signatures have been identified and published. These types of systems produce fewer false positives than signature analysis types, but the time involved in updating these systems tends to be greater, because it takes longer to design and identify new protocol analysis data.

An IDS or NIDS may show that someone has gotten into your system, how that person got in, and when. It can't, however, tell you what the intruder may have done while inside. This is where tools called system integrity verifiers (SIVs) come in. An SIV can be used to compare checksums of files before and after intrusion, to see if there have been any changes.

A checksum is a numeric value that is calculated based on the specific characters and their positions in every line of a program. A change in a single character or spacing will produce a markedly different checksum, so calculating these values is a fast way of determining if anything about a program has been changed.

> A checksum is a numeric value that is calculated based on the specific characters and their positions in every line of a program.

An SIV may also be used to find instances of privilege escalation, such as when a legitimate user with a lower level of privilege acquires root or administrator status. A privilege escalation is often a precursor to illegal activity, and would certainly be a serious breach of policy in any appropriate security environment.

The developers of all of these intrusion detection tools, like developers of virus detection tools, face the never-ending task of trying to keep current with the exploits of intruders or attackers. But as we saw with BIND, new vulnerabilities and attack possibilities are discovered continually, and any tool's effectiveness is only as good as its last update. If you've got detection tools that are well supported with current signatures, you have a much better chance of detecting an intrusion and knowing how to "aim" your response.

# RESPONSE

Left to their own devices, your people will usually under-react or overreact to confirmation of an attack or intrusion. Some will want to pull the plug, immediately; others will be in denial or stalled by indecision. It's not fair to your people, to yourself, or to your company to leave the response part of the security equation undefined. The most stringent security technologies cannot bolster response in the face of vague procedures and inconsistent oversight.

So, what should you do? What would be the effect on the business of pulling the plug under a particular circumstance? Would it be better to simply try to selectively close off some ports, redirect an attack, or try to confine the attack to one area, while permitting limited performance access in others? These are all possibilities, but choosing one should be an informed decision involving business unit stakeholders, IT managers, and security personnel.

**It's not fair to your people, to yourself, or to your company to leave the response part of the security equation undefined.**

The following are some guidelines for an incident response team. The specifics need to be tailored to your company's unique characteristics.

First of all, security and information risk management should be an executive-level-inspired endeavor. You must identify an executive whose responsibility it is to handle high-level security issues. Therefore, the decision to pull the plug at an online securities Web site should be made by a C-level executive, not by someone monitoring the network console.

Your human resources department should be represented on the incident response team, because the odds are much greater that an employee rather than an outsider is mounting the attack.

Your IT or MIS group should also be involved, not because security should be its responsibility, but because security personnel may discover a compromised MIS system.

Now is the time to think about which outsiders to include; it's too late to do so during an attack. According to Ellen Hancock at Exodus, its data centers have facilities that can prevent a physical intruder's exit, and the local authorities have guaranteed a four-minute or shorter response time to a man-trap alert. Network attacks are crimes, and they need to be reported to local authorities or the FBI. Your incident response team should not be calling 911 during an attack. They should have a name and phone number of someone who, through prearrangement, is expecting to be contacted under such circumstances.

Of course, your security personnel should be key members of the incident response team. They can help decide who should have responsibility based on the type and severity of an attack.

With your incident response team defined, you need to develop a response procedure—what to do and whom to call. It will cover kinds of incidents, kinds of responses, and chains of command. It will also cover logging and auditing, as well as preservation of evidence.

One of the most important parts of the process is practice. The incident response team must be trained on the entire procedure, and the training should include dry runs and periodic drills. Microsoft's Howard Schmidt makes a kind of competition out of it. "The red team [his security team] will conduct a mock exploit, and our employees are encouraged to find out who has been attacked," he explained. "The ones who find attempted intrusions get awards. It keeps everyone appropriately focused on security."

## Manage the Risk

We've already described several ways that intruders can get into your system. Remember, today's trusted security component is tomorrow's Swiss cheese. (Just think about BIND, for example.) You can mitigate the preponderance of holes by conducting a thorough assessment. And you can keep things relatively secure by staying on top of newly discovered vulnerabilities and their fixes. If you have information that absolutely must remain secure, then you must not distribute that information over your enterprise network, your virtual private network, or (gulp) the Internet.

Developers of IDS or NIDS systems play the same game of leapfrog that virus makers play with virus-protection products and their companies. Your virus protection looks for known virus signatures and typical virus activities. As new viruses are incubated, new codes must be added to your virus-protection software. In a similar way, the IDS and NIDS systems look for known exploit signatures and activities. These, too, need to be updated frequently to keep them as current as possible. These are endemic holes in any intrusion detection system. You can increase your odds of preventing an attack by staying up-to-date.

Some incident response procedures call for informing associated companies that may have a presence on the affected Web site. However, if the attack is actually coming from that other Web site, the alert information is falling right into the intruder's hands. Alerts should be sent via other communications systems, such as telephones, pagers, and the like. This helps to keep information out of the wrong hands.

**Alerts should be sent via other communications systems, such as telephones, pagers, and the like. This helps to keep information out of the wrong hands.**

## THERE'S NO DISCRIMINATION

There's a law of averages at play in cyberspace. There are many millions of Web sites and even more millions of people browsing the Web. If entropy were factored in, there would be an average of three visitors per Web site at any given time. But disorder rules in cyberspace. Some Web sites are visited by millions; others are visited by none (on average). Among the visitors is an unknown number of crackers. Their percentage of the total cyber population is very small. Nevertheless, with the appropriate tools (e.g., war dialers and scanning software), they can scope out the Web to an extent that is disproportionate to their numbers.

Here's how the law of averages plays out. A cracker with a purposeful target in mind is likely to go after a big-name site. That accounts for the thousands of attacks being beaten off by Microsoft, for example. Less conspicuous Web sites seem to be relatively safe from such attackers. But many attackers have no specific targets in mind. They just look for targets that appear vulnerable, and cast their nets over the whole space. To these people, small is not invisible. Any Web site may end up in their crosshairs.

Perpetrators of computer crime don't discriminate. The only difference is in the visibility of the media response. National media do not cover stories of local ISPs whose servers have been breached. You have to dig hard to find those stories. On the other hand, every time someone sneezes in a Microsoft data center, the media say "gesundheit."

Recently an intrusion was reported at the elite World Economic Forum in Davos, Switzerland. Apparently, a group protesting the gathering penetrated the Forum's Web server and copied a list of 27,000 names, email addresses, and credit card numbers. This gathering usually includes heads of state, prominent CEOs, bankers, artists, educators, and journalists. Thus, any attack on its Web site is guaranteed to receive lots of exposure.

Soon after the incident, Swiss authorities were poring over logs, looking for who got in, when, and how. The process requires care, especially if the exploit went undetected while it was occurring. Knowledgeable intruders have ways of erasing logs and covering their tracks, and those are usually the last few tasks that are carried out. Most intruders hope to enjoy a repeat performance, so it is common for them to take steps to eliminate evidence of their visit.

### Small but Not Invisible

Here is a brief history of a security breach at the Lightlink Web site. You've probably never read about it in newspapers or magazines. Lightlink is a local ISP that was started in 1995 and serves a base of 2,500 subscribers in the Ithaca, New York area (near Cornell University). In 1996, on a Friday, the founder and Web master, Homer Wilson Smith, received an anonymous email message from a hacker who had gained access to a user's account using a stolen password. "He told us which account he used, but not how he got the password," said Smith.

The hacker did go on to tell Lightlink that he had managed to get root access (highest level control) using a system command that Smith created for some of Lightlink's users. "The command allows them to restart the Web server when it is jammed," he explained. The intruder gave Smith details of how he achieved root access and advised him to check the system for similar scripts. The intruder also asked Smith to destroy the email message in return for the information, and Smith did so.

Sure enough, the exploit worked exactly as described. Smith went ahead and fixed both that command and a few others he had created and forgotten about. Then he locked the account that the hacker had entered from, and informed the user about the intrusion.

But Smith wondered whether the hacker had been completely forthcoming. "We were naturally suspicious that maybe he'd left some back doors in the system just for fun," he recalled. So the staff did a sweep of the Lightlink Web site, using the oldest system binaries they had on backup tapes. First, they loaded the backup tapes onto a hard drive so that the directory structure matched the then-current version. Then, they wrote a program to compare the hard drive code with the then-present code. This is similar to what an SIV tool does in determining whether there have been any changes to a system.

Hidden deep in the system binary directories, Smith found a file called logfile.dat that contained a long list of user names and clear-text passwords. This is known as a "rootkit," a hacker tool used for accumulating passwords.

In that rootkit directory, Smith also found a number of backed-up copies of login, ps (process stats), ifconfig (interface config), and netstat (network stats)—important system programs used to monitor various system resources. "All of these programs had been replaced by hacked versions," said Smith, "and I presumed he'd backed up the unhacked versions in order to clean up and leave without a trace later."

It was a simple matter to put things right by comparing the backed-up versions to known good versions, then replacing the hacked versions. "This guy was good," Smith admitted. "He had surgically altered all the timestamps to look just like they did when first installed in October 1994."

The hacked login program was designed to keep a clear-text record in a log file each time someone logged into the Lightlink network as a shell user. It also had a back door, with its own password, permitting the intruder to get at a root shell at any time.

The hacked ps, ifconfig, and netstat programs were each modified so they would not reveal certain processes carried out by the intruder (thus covering the hacker's tracks), and they would not log the root logins in a variety of databases that normally keep track of who logs in and when.

"This hacker had complete access to the system," Smith informed us. "We assume the hacker got the encrypted password file plus access to everyone's home directories, mail, and Web and FTP sites, as someone with root access can do." Lightlink found no evidence of packet sniffing on remote systems. If they had, it could have meant compromised passwords for anyone using telnet from Lightlink to any-where else. "Of course, we took immediate steps to tighten Lightlink security, but this process is a never-ending battle," Smith lamented.

## Big and Very Tempting

Does this happen to big companies too? We need look no further than Microsoft's plight of late. Getting into Microsoft's network is considered a feather in the cap for any cracker, and as Microsoft's Schmidt intimated, that sys-tem beats back many thousands of attempts each week.

The security chief of another big company, an Exodus customer, called Exodus last year to say he was concerned. "A lead programmer was leaving and muttering something about 'getting even,'" Exodus CEO Hancock began. The Exodus security team went right into action, and the first thing they found was that this individual had already changed the root key and given his former company the wrong one. "So we had to hack the root key, which took us 15 minutes," Hancock chuckled. As soon as they got into the system, they found the programmer was currently attempting to connect remotely to the system. "We would shut down one port, and he'd attempt to connect through another port," Hancock remembered.

"We kept playing this game until we finally shut him out entirely. Then we patched the system, locking the door permanently," she said, smiling with satisfaction. Afterward, the Exodus security team went on to look for changes, much as the Lightlink team had done, and to undo whatever modifications and insertions had been made by the disgruntled former employee.

## JUST THE TIP OF THE ICEBERG

Are these isolated stories? Not at all. In fact, Gartner Group reported that 90 percent of organizations that contracted for external security assessments have discovered significant vulnerabilities. And 80 percent of Gartner's own research clients either have, or believe they have, been victims of security breaches.

> **Gartner Group reported that 90 percent of organizations that contracted for external security assessments have discovered significant vulnerabilities.**

In 1997, the FBI and the Computer Security Institute reported that 42 percent of respondents to a query had experienced unauthorized use of their systems within the last year. Of that group, 32 percent admitted to losses that totaled over $100 million in aggregate.

As we said earlier, even the tough get broken. Last year, when Mafiaboy was attacking the likes of eBay, Yahoo!, and E*Trade, someone else was attacking the Web site registered to RSA Security, Inc. This is the company whose marketing slogan is "The Most Trusted Name in e-Security." Those who visited the Web site that Sunday morning found the home page defaced, and alongside the company logo were the words: "RSA Security Inc. Hacked. Trust us with your data! Praise Allah! The most trusted name in e-Security has been owned. Big things are coming."

In May 2000, about 160 CIA employees were informed about the investigation of their by-invitation-only chat room, which happened to reside on that agency's classified computer system. These spy-agency employees used the chat room to swap off-color jokes and other comments. And the investigation went undetected for five years!

Not every crime gets reported, either. A Taiwan bank, for example, had NT$50 million stolen by a hacker who got into its computer system and successfully transferred the funds to a foreign savings account. The bank in question, though, did not report the theft because of concerns about its credit rating and reputation. A large U.S. bank was forthcoming about a group of Russian crackers who had penetrated its electronic money transfer system in 1996 and, over four months, had transferred more than $10 million to a variety of international accounts.

### Publicity You Don't Need

Web crimes are big news. The media has a field day with each new exploit. Big companies appear powerless, and 15-year-olds appear powerful (but misguided). That's the type of publicity your company doesn't need.

What you don't read or hear about are the companies that fend off hundreds or thousands of penetration attempts, or the companies that discover an intrusion in progress and limit the attacker's ability to do damage. These are the companies that have all the parts of the security system working together. These are the companies that make it appropriately difficult to penetrate their sites, and are able to detect and track intrusions in the few instances when they occur. These are the companies that have incident response teams who know what to look for, what to do, and whom to call.

# PART IV

# The Underpinnings

*This chapter and the next provide a technical framework for understanding security issues.*

# CHAPTER 7

# Assessing the Security Risk

When has technology alone ever solved a business problem? Has any company ever simply plugged in a computer, installed some applications, and ended up with a tailored solution to a business or operations requirement? Think about your current business system. Did it involve input from sales, accounting, management, and production? Of course it did. Did it involve system analysis? Certainly. Yet many companies still approach security as a fundamental technology problem in need of a technology solution.

There are no off-the-rack security solutions. Like a capable business system, an enterprise security solution should be built upon business objectives and cultural and organizational factors. A security solution that forces your company to change its behavior to fit the solution's characteristics simply will not work.

There is far more to a security risk assessment than looking for holes in system, network, and application software. It begins by taking a look at risk, defined as:

$$\text{Risk} = \text{Asset Value} \times \text{Threat} \times \text{Vulnerability}$$

❑ **Asset Value** is the importance of an information asset to the firm's strategy.

❑ **Threats** are events or actions that could have a negative impact on the availability, integrity, or confidentiality of an information asset.

❑ **Vulnerabilities** are the absence, inadequacy, or inconsistency of facilities and processes that are deployed to protect the asset's value from the identified threats.

One could evaluate the vulnerabilities of an enterprise network and find many of the opportunities for attacking it. But the problem with that approach is that it lacks context. It focuses on technology without regard to people and process. It makes no distinctions about asset values and threats. We would argue that the outcome of such an exercise leaves a company's security understanding seriously deficient. A true security risk assessment must address asset values, threats, and vulnerabilities.

One of a CEO's most important functions is overseeing the corporation's management of risk. We assert that security—and its information-management

> **One of a CEO's most important functions is overseeing the corporation's management of risk. We assert that security—and its information-management implications—should be part of that risk-management portfolio.**

implications—should be part of that risk-management portfolio.

How vulnerable is your enterprise to unauthorized access, tampering, and theft? Here are the questions that need answers:

❏ What is your information worth? (asset value)
❏ Who might benefit from access to that information? (threats)
❏ What protects access to that information, and how secure are those protections? (vulnerabilities)

The more your information is worth, the greater the number of threats, and the broader your spectrum of vulnerability, the more risk you have to manage.

Insurance companies determine drivers' accident risk exposure by their activities and characteristics—how much they drive, where they drive, and so on. We believe your company's risk exposure is also directly related to its activities, and your security solution should be driven, in part, by that activities base. Suppose your company had a preponderance of IP packets (associated with LAN and Internet traffic). Would it make sense, then, to spend as much on securing IPX packets (5 percent of network traffic) as on IP packets (90 percent of traffic)? We don't think so.

If you focused more attention on internal security (80 percent likely source of attack) than on remote intrusion (20 percent likely source of attack), wouldn't that make sense? We think so, and so does VeriSign's CEO Stratton Sclavos.

"We've seen the proportion of insider to outsider attacks going down because more companies are paying more attention to it," he suggested. "The vetting process in our data centers is very stringent, and we look at credit history as carefully as we do a legal history, to weed out susceptibility to bribery," he explained. According to Sclavos, the job of security has gotten a lot harder. "Before the Internet, you just had to make sure your enterprise was isolated. Now, you have to make sure everything you have is available to everyone who needs it, on an individual need-to-know basis. Talk about monumental tasks."

## INFORMATION ASSET VALUE

Not all information is equal. For example, if employee name and phone extension information was made public, it may create some problems with unsolicited headhunter calls, but it doesn't put you at immediate competitive risk. Sales contact information, though, is more valuable and it would be damaging to your company if that data got into the wrong hands. Intellectual property and trade secrets are the crown jewels, and have the most influence on your risk profile.

**Not all information is equal.**

Yet, none of this information is evaluated and shown as an asset on a balance sheet. How does one value information? The answer is, qualitatively. Without needing to be precise, you can establish relative values. For example, human resource information may have about one-tenth the value of sales contact information, and one-hundredth the value of IP and trade secret information. This, at least, gives you a context for comparing the risk posed by various types of information. It will be important later, when you are creating or modifying policies and procedures.

# THREATS

About 95 percent of recent stories on Web crimes focused on outsiders disrupting Web site operations, or getting in and copying sensitive information. Yet, as we've mentioned, most reported incidents involve insiders. Therefore, a security environment aimed primarily at preventing outsider intrusions is likely to be blindsided.

Outsider threats include script kiddies, competitors, extortionists, and thieves. The largest number are the script kiddies, who get kudos for breaking and entering but are usually clueless about the comparative values of your information. Competitors, on the other hand, are much fewer in number but know very well what your information is worth. Extortionists want to kidnap your information and ransom it back to you; thieves want to sell your information to the highest bidder.

Insider threats include disgruntled employees, former employees with a grudge, model employees who have run up huge gambling debts, and employees who are planning to leave and to work for one of your competitors. Not all employees have equal access to your information, so you need to qualify the insider threats by the levels of access categories your employees have. For example, at first glance, your receptionist is less of a risk than, say, your chief design engineer. But if that receptionist manages to get network administrator privileges, all bets are off. And that's where vulnerabilities fit in.

# VULNERABILITIES

Can someone slip a piece of paper over an electronic door sensor and gain entry to a restricted area? This is what Exodus Communications discovered when it ran a comprehensive security exercise at its facility. Is the bulletproof glass with which you surround your data center effective against both gun and rifle bullets? Exodus learned from security experts that there are differences in bulletproof glass.

What happens if someone barges past a reception area? What barriers do you have to keep an intruder contained? What kinds of information can a salesperson store in his or her laptop computer? Do you shred most paper documents before discarding them? Are your accounts receivable records duplicated and stored off-site? (A disgruntled employee once put a company out of business by erasing the accounts payable files and the on-site backup files.) Are your data center, servers, routers, and switches located in an area with access restrictions?

Notice that none of these questions involved network operations. If we concentrated our assessment on network specifics, we could easily miss a lot of other vulnerabilities.

The network is important, but it needs to be assessed within the context of these other vulnerabilities.

## NETWORK VULNERABILITIES

Network vulnerabilities are where many assessment projects both start and stop. Remember, your network is only one part of the overall vulnerability spectrum.

Think of your enterprise network as a castle surrounded by a moat. The castle contains all the computers, servers, switches, and routers that constitute your enterprise network. The moat is there to keep unauthorized outsiders out. The drawbridge can be lowered, however, to permit outsiders in (e.g., allow external network packets to flow in), or to let them pass requests to the insiders (e.g., pass packets to a proxy server on the outside which passes the information inside).

> **Think of your enterprise network as a castle surrounded by a moat.**

If the drawbridge were always down and no one checked outsiders' credentials, then the castle and its occupants would be extremely vulnerable. This is the case when an enterprise network is attached to the Internet without a firewall. The firewall, or firewall and proxy server, represents the drawbridge that can be raised and lowered to prevent unauthorized outsider access.

Your enterprise network vulnerabilities fall into two categories: outsiders trying to get in, and insiders trying to escalate their information access privileges. An outsider who gets in also becomes an insider, and also tries to escalate his or her information access privileges.

### Casing the Joint

A serious attacker of whatever stripe will do his or her homework before unwrapping the burglar tools. This is akin to a bank robber checking out a bank in an inconspicuous way.

> **A serious attacker of whatever stripe will do his or her homework before unwrapping the burglar tools.**

There are many things to be learned about your network without first having to try its doors and windows. Your Web site itself may offer many clues as to what lies behind that home page. These include domain names, network blocks, and IP addresses. Other resources, such as the InterNIC database (a database containing information related to domain name registration), will list your registered domain information and the name of your registered network manager. In addition, press releases posted on the site can provide an attacker with information about partner companies and potential alternative ways in.

### Remote Checking for Open Doors

Outsiders are located beyond the moat and the castle walls, but they want to find out as much as possible about what things are like inside. So they'll send messages inside to try to ferret out that information. An IP address is like the address of an apartment building, and ports are like the doors to individual apartments. Thus, once attackers discover an active IP address, they begin looking for open ports.

A *ping* is a tool used by network technicians to determine whether a server is live. It is part of the TCP/IP protocol, and involves sending an ICMP ECHO packet to the system being probed to find out whether that system will respond with an ICMP ECHO_REPLY packet. (Remember the "Smurf" attack?)

Usually, insiders use pings to check on the health of the enterprise system. But to a firewall in default mode, an outside ping seems perfectly in order. In fact, unless specifically told not to, a firewall will allow outside ping packets to come in. So it lets that message pass on through, and lets the response message go back out. An ECHO_REPLY tells the outsider that the system is live, and that's valuable information. So a firewall that doesn't block external ICMP packets makes the network more vulnerable to attack.

Therefore, one part of a network vulnerability assessment is to check for things like whether an outsider can easily ping IP addresses inside the network. A thorough vulnerability assessment uses the same kinds of tools that crackers use to probe and gather information. The assessors uses these tools in the same ways as a would-be cracker. The idea is to find the same holes

**One part of a network vulnerability assessment is to check for things like whether an outsider can easily ping IP addresses inside the network.**

a potential intruder would find. The objective is to find them first, and eliminate them, if possible.

## Insider Network Security Assessment

As we said earlier, an outsider who finds a remote access into the network becomes an insider. So the next order of business is to find the vulnerabilities to insider escalations of privileges.

A favorite target of crackers is a list of user names and passwords. Some popular operating systems, in default configurations, make it rather easy to get such lists. A variety of tools has been developed for matching user names to their easily cracked passwords. An assessor, or a cracker, who has an ID and password has a key to a door that could lead to the vault.

Several excellent books are available that detail the known vulnerabilities of Unix and Windows NT operating systems. Two examples are *The Complete Guide to Internet Security*, Merkow and Breithaupt and *Secrets & Lies: Digital Security in a Networked World*, Schneier. Assessors have access to such books, and so do crackers. You can assume that a good network vulnerability assessment will include a by-the-numbers check to make sure that if your system has such vulnerabilities, they have been, or can be, patched or otherwise mitigated.

Remember that books about specific attack exploits become obsolete very quickly. The preferred assessors augment their books of tricks with the most recent information about new exploits. These are available from several Web sites, and new sources are appearing all the time.

## The Keys to the Kingdom

The ultimate goal of any cracker is to gain root access. With root access, a person has carte-blanche control of the system and entry to any and all of its files. Assessors who can get the keys to the system, so to speak, will do mischief and create changes in their wake. Then they will assess whether the existing security environment is capable of detecting that intrusion and identifying changes that were wrought.

> The ultimate goal of any cracker is to gain root access. With root access, a person has carte-blanche control of the system and entry to any and all of its files.

Obviously, the assessor and your company must agree as to which areas are off limits so that no irreversible damage is done to critical information. (But you won't have that same cooperation from a cracker.) So to some extent, even an excellent assessor is somewhat constrained, and final results will not be absolutely comprehensive.

The network vulnerability assessment, in conjunction with the asset value and threat assessments, provides all the variables with which to evaluate your information security risk. But there is one exception: Your vulnerability to DoS or DDoS attacks is particularly hard to qualify.

Both during and after a DoS or DDoS attack, your information assets are in no danger, but other soft assets are. The trust your customers have that your Web site will be available at all times is temporarily crushed when the wheels come screeching to a halt. Even if the wheels don't stop, but continue to turn very slowly, you risk the frustration of your customers, loss of business, and loss of prestige. By factoring in that DoS or DDoS risk, though you may have little control over that vulnerability, you will be better able to manage the risk.

What are these attacks, and why can't you prevent them? The answer is that a DoS or DDoS attack makes use of authorized processes to pervert the service you provide to customers.

## DENIAL OF SERVICE ATTACKS

Damaging attacks do not all involve intrusion. In fact, some of the more costly and disruptive attacks in 2000 were DoS and DDoS types. In neither instance was a target Web site penetrated. They were simply incapacitated. But a popular e-commerce site can lose millions of dollars when legitimate users are denied access, or an auction site, such as eBay, is faced with disgruntled buyers and sellers.

What does a DoS or DDoS attack look like to a hapless user? It looks like the Web site is either operating very slowly, or not operating at all. Now, this situation can happen without a DoS attack if a Web site has become a focus of huge interest and many more visitors than anticipated are all trying to get connected. But when a Web site has been targeted for attack, it is just one visitor—the attacker—who is causing all the mayhem.

There are several varieties of DoS attack, but they all try to either consume bandwidth or tie up target system resources by flooding a Web site with incoming packets. The previously described Smurf attack was a bandwidth consumer. If there are 100 systems on that network, the target system will be inundated with 100 ECHO_REPLY packets for each initial ICMP ECHO packet. If there are 1,000 systems on the network, 1,000 ECHO packets will soon be hurtling toward the spoofed target server. It is easy to see how quickly such an attack can humble even an industrial-strength target system.

## A SYN Flood Attack

Another DoS variety is called a "SYN flood" attack. It takes advantage of TCP's mechanism for establishing connections. Just like a telephone call, when you click on a URL, your system sends a "Hello, is this Joe?" message (a SYN packet). The server on the other end sends a "Yes, this is Joe" message in return (a SYN/ACK packet). Then your system sends a "Hi, Joe, this is Sue" ACK packet. Then the two systems communicate.

Typically, most systems allocate a relatively small amount of resources (memory and processor cycles) for handling potential connections. Thus, if dozens or more SYN packets flow in at roughly the same time, they can easily exhaust those allocated resources. This is especially true if the SYN packets are spoofed with a nonexistent source address. In that case, the second system replies with SYN/ACK packets to that nonexistent address. While that second system waits for ACK replies (that will never come), it has to reserve resources for those connections. An incoming flood of SYN packets continues to tie up more and more resources, and the system is quickly inundated and hobbled.

Effective countermeasures have been developed that can identify and redirect attacks that appear to come from the same (spoofed) source address. As a result, attackers became creative and invented the DDoS attack.

## A DDoS Attack

In a DDoS attack, such as those that were unleashed on major Web sites in February 2000, the attacker must first create an army of zombie systems that can be remotely controlled. By intruding into and establishing covert control of several systems having discrete source addresses, the attacker sets them all up to flood a target system with SYN packets. But the source addresses are all different, reflecting the source addresses of the zombie systems. Ordinary SYN-flood countermeasures see a flood of requests but they are coming from several rather than one source system. It looks no different from a peak-period rush of SYN packets. Soon the volume far exceeds such a rush, but by then the gates are open and the cows are gone.

A DDoS attack can be fended off, but it takes a lot of effort. In July 2000, a security team at a large southeastern university did just that. In the weeks prior to the attack the security team noticed strange outages on the 40,000-machine campus network. As they described it, "Systems that were normally rock-steady were dropping sessions. Packet losses approached 30 percent on some switches. And the problems occurred at random times and for varying durations."

With the outbreak of another series of packet losses and unreturned pings, the team isolated the problem to one section of the network located in one campus building. They immediately deployed IDS probes on that network segment. With the probe activated, they launched a tool that provides statistics on bandwidth, packet size, and TCP/UDP port usage. That showed them what was happening. Normally, network traffic is divided among the most frequently used services, such as the Web, email, and so on. What they saw was completely different. Every port below number 1024 was in use, each had equal byte and packet counts, and the counts were rapidly increasing as the team watched. During a respite in the attack, the team had analyzed the offending packets and set up another IDS tool that would quickly alert them should another wave of packets begin to hit.

Two hours later, the new IDS began beeping them; the culprit was a SYN flood attack. But unlike a typical DDoS case, in which attackers and targets are widely separated, here the attackers and targets were confined to one IP subnet (a small network section). The attacking system was spoofing the source addresses, creating that extended wait for the second ACK packet. With 300 machines on that network segment, the team was unable to quickly determine which hosts had been compromised.

Using the new IDS tool, though, they were able to determine that their network's rogue machines were being controlled from a computer in Europe. They quickly configured the Internet router with ingress/egress filters to block the packets from the controlling host. The attack was thwarted.

In this case, the team had more than a DDoS attack to deal with. Their own systems were being used as both zombies and targets. That meant that in addition to service denial, they were also dealing with penetration. The next steps, of course, were to identify the compromised hosts and use an SIV tool to find and undo any changes or additions (e.g., Trojans, new applications, etc.) to those hosts.

## ATTACK-DIVERTING TECHNOLOGIES

Arbor Networks, Asta Networks, and Mazu Networks are all attempting to tackle DoS assaults. All three offer devices that sit close to routers and detect, trace, and block those attacks. The idea is to *prescreen incoming packets, and divert those that are suspicious,* removing that burden from the router. That, in turn, leaves the router free to route legitimate packets. The hoped-for results will be fewer successful intrusions with little or no impact on traffic routing efficiency and throughput. Arbor's system is being put through its paces by Merit Networks, and Exodus is testing the other two.

Bill Hancock, Exodus' chief technical officer, believes *isolating the filtering function from the router* makes sense. Exodus will compare the results to those achieved using its internally developed techniques, such as using a dedicated high-speed switch to redirect suspicious packets to a dead-end IP address.

## ALL ASSESSMENTS ARE NOT EQUAL

Human judgment plays a key part in an assessment. One expert may do a far better job of uncovering information during the casing-of-the-joint phase. Another expert may be more creative in the use of assessment tools.

Whether assessing asset values, threats, or vulnerabilities, the more thorough the assessment, the better the risk evaluation. When it comes to people, process, and network vulnerabilities, it may seem easier to be like an ostrich and bury your head in the ground. If you don't look, you won't find anything unpleasant, right?

125

But if you're going to look, then look thoroughly. You won't find all the holes in your system, but you'll find a lot of them.

# CHAPTER 8

# Your Enterprise Security Architecture

A risk assessment should be a beginning, not an end. It's analogous to having a full physical examination—blood test, static and dynamic EKG, visual inspection, palpation, and the like. The tests find systemic problem areas, but they cannot examine environmental and lifestyle causalities. It's the physician who looks at the examination results and tries to correlate them with things like exercise, diet, genetic predispositions, and stress. Your doctor may prescribe medication that can immediately lower blood pressure or cholesterol levels, and a thorough  physician will suggest dietary and lifestyle changes that can improve your health.

In many ways, the outset of an enterprise security architecture (ESA) effort is similar to your physician looking over the blood test and EKG results. You are looking for trouble signs. Some problems can be remedied quickly. Others may require a more

In many ways, the outset of an ESA effort is similar to your physician looking over the blood test and EKG results. You are looking for trouble signs.

complex series of steps. All actions are aimed at improving your security profile, in the short term.

The ESA approach must look beyond your current business processes and vulnerabilities, and envision what your future state will need to be in order to meet your future objectives. With those beginning and end states in view, you can plan the most effective and efficient series of changes required for making that transition.

An ESA methodology is a structured process for designing and planning enterprise security capabilities that effec-

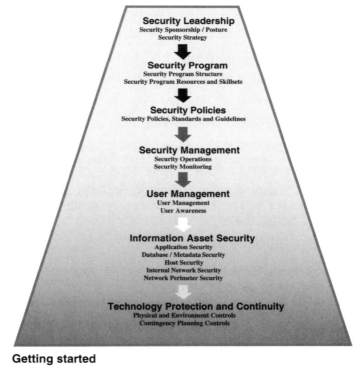

**Getting started**

*figure 8-1    Enterprise Security Model*

tively support and enable business strategy and objectives. It should involve best practices, guidelines, approaches, tools, and techniques. And it should be founded on the principle of automating processes where possible, consolidating processes where logical, and eliminating redundancies and waste.

An ESA effort is a top-down process that begins with security leadership and drives the layers below (see the model in Figure 8-1). Unlike the Open-System Interconnect (OSI) model that divides networked computing into seven independent and encapsulated layers, this model's layers are interdependent. That means changes in one area, such as security policies, are likely to evoke changes in other areas, such as security management.

## GETTING STARTED

The natural starting point for establishing an ESA is the just-completed risk assessment. Review and analyze it, identifying systemic problems and assessing their potential impact on your business operations.

Let's look as an example at the outset of an ESA process for Acme Corporation (not its real name). Right away, Acme found two problems. First, its network staff consisted of four employees, only one of whom (the manager) had knowledge of the overall architecture. The other three had knowledge about specific areas of the network, but lacked knowledge of the whole, and there was no formal mechanism for knowledge transfer.

Second, there was significant network personnel turn-over. What had been an eleven-person department a year before was reduced to four through turnover.

Diving down into system specifics, Acme Corporation analyzed five network areas:

❑ network switches,
❑ network performance and protocols,
❑ network services analysis,
❑ internal DNS analysis, and
❑ network management tools.

Acme's system included 34 switches handling mostly 10 Mbps Ethernet and 100 Mbps Fast Ethernet network transfers. All devices were connected through an Asynchronous Transfer Mode (ATM) core, and all traffic had to pass through the PowerHub before routing.

Although Acme Corporation's bandwidth requirements are fully met by this network configuration, this architecture poses a potential network bottleneck as well as a single point of potential network failure (the PowerHub).

Acme also found several instances of default "null" user names and passwords (user names or passwords that were left blank and were therefore not preventing access) on their switches, making them vulnerable to unauthorized access to switch configurations.

## Activities-Based Analysis

By analyzing data gathered by the protocol and performance analysis tool, Acme found that IP, IPX, NetBEUI, RIP,

DECnet, LAT, and OSI protocols all existed on its network. This was the case despite the company's data indicating that IP (associated with LAN and Internet networking), IPX (associated with Novell NetWare), and SNA (associated with IBM networks) were the only protocols allowed on the network. Thus, there were five unauthorized protocols in the mix, and the tool detected no SNA traffic at all. Since every protocol has its own unique and published vulnerabilities, the more protocols on a network, the higher the risk. The majority of traffic was IP (90 percent); IPX accounted for only 5 percent, NetBEUI for 3 percent, and the remaining protocols for an aggregate of 2 percent.

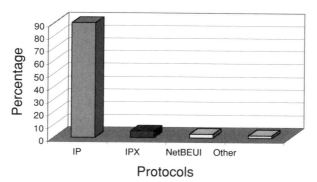

figure 8-2    Acme's network traffic consisted of these
percentages of traffic categorized by protocol.

Most of the IP traffic was NetBIOS over IP used for LAN file and printer sharing. The IPX traffic was used for client file and printer connectivity to Novell NetWare servers, and for NetBIOS connectivity to Windows NT servers. Acme also found a high number of broadcast packets on the network during its analysis. Most of it was Novell's Service

Advertising Protocol (SAP) or Microsoft Networking broad-
casts. Novell's Routing Information Protocol (RIP) was also
observed on the network.

As a result of the analysis, Acme's initial set of changes
were:

Remove NetBEUI from all devices. It is not a secure
protocol and can cause network performance degrada-
tion.

Configure filters on the backbone router and edge
devices to limit the amount of network broadcast traffic. This would increase overall network performance
and reduce the risk of a broadcast-style DoS attack.

Configure all network devices with a default gateway
to eliminate the need for RIP on the network backbone.
RIP has security vulnerabilities and can be used to redirect traffic to untrusted devices.

Ultimately migrate all devices to an IP-only environment. Properly implemented, IP-only networks are
inherently more secure than networks having multiple
protocols.

## Lots of Potentially Open Doors

Many operating systems support a variety of services, and
many of these services are notoriously vulnerable. Acme
Corporation's network was found to have a large number of
undocumented devices providing uncontrolled network services (see Figure 8-3).

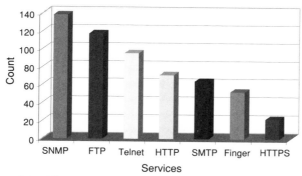

*figure 8-3*    *These were some of the uncontrolled network services*
*found on Acme's network. Many of them,*
*in the hands of crackers, are notoriously vulnerable.*

There are sets of services in the TCP/IP suite that have little or no security associated with them, and that are common targets for those who would intrude. These services could allow unauthorized access to information on hosts and the loss or corruption of sensitive data, such as user names and passwords. Furthermore, these services can be exploited for launching downstream attacks both on and off the network. Thus, Acme Corporation took the following steps:

❏ Developed detailed policies and procedures that specify which network services are allowed on the network, and implemented compliance monitoring.

❏ Consolidated and limited common IP services to the smallest number of secure intranet services. Centralized intranet resource servers should provide all internal FTP and HTTP services.

❏ Clearly delineated workstations and servers. Desktop systems have no robust security features and should not be used as servers.

❏ Disabled all services not explicitly needed for business. Consolidated and centralized servers that route SMTP mail both internally and externally. This allows Acme Corporation to enforce policies and procedures on the use of email.

Acme's current internal DNS server configuration permits any host on the network to obtain a complete copy of the DNS table using "zone transfers," a common vulnerability. As a result, Acme Corporation:

❏ Configured the DNS servers to allow zone transfer only from authorized hosts.

❏ Created policies and procedures detailing proper configuration and maintenance of the DNS tables, including change-management procedures for adding and removing hosts.

❏ Ensured that DNS tables are all up to date and monitored for compliance.

With regard to network management tools, Acme Corporation discovered that more than 100 devices on the network were running the Simple Network Management Protocol (SNMP). The default on most systems makes SNMP public, permitting unauthorized users to gain sensitive information about network devices and to change device configuration. Acme Corporation took the following action:

❏ Changed the default SNMP community string from "public" to a more secure string containing uppercase and lowercase letters, numbers, and non-dictionary words.

❏ Changed the SNMP community string from "Openview" to a more secure string, as above.

❏ Set up a dedicated network management station configured with existing management tools.

While this example is not exhaustive, it illustrates how a company can use risk assessment findings to make immediate and short-term remedial changes to its systems.


## CURRENT-STATE BASELINING

Current-state baselining is an ambitious process step. It must involve the company's business-unit and technology leaders, as well as security-focused personnel. Scrutinize organization charts, network diagrams, and technologies. Review the policies for security, IT operations and management, and user-management. These policies must then be factored in with any system considerations.

One of your objectives is to understand the corporate values that are delivered by technologies. For example, in the case of Amazon.com, one corporate value might be personalization, which is delivered via a combination of database and heuristic software technologies. Another company might provide extremely fast user account updating through a combination of real-time software and fast database servers.

**One of your objectives is to understand the corporate values that are delivered by technologies.**

Another objective is to evaluate those technology threats that could have an impact on your company's ability to deliver and maintain compelling value. Consider eBay, whose value to sellers is providing continuous processing of buyer bidding, and to buyers is providing an enormous choice of auction items. Web technology is critical to that value proposition, and a DDoS attack would be devastating to eBay.

At the conclusion of this phase, develop risk and risk mitigation measurement metrics, and create a current-state baseline table of risks resulting from assets, threats, and vulnerabilities.

## ENVISIONING YOUR FUTURE STATE

In attempting to envision your future state, there are several possibilities. One is to simply restructure the existing security environment to remedy the remaining areas of vulnerabilities. Another is to examine the company's strategic priorities to see how they may affect the business model and future operations. With these in mind, the current baseline model should be examined not only to see what can be done to make it more effective, but to explore how it can be modified or expanded to meet the security requirements of strategic changes in business and operations.

Working together with business-unit and technology leaders, security-focused personnel, and the other resources you used in coming up with your current-state baseline, you should establish alternatives in several areas. These include:

information security strategy, the information security program structure, roles, responsibilities, processors, resources, and skill sets.

Rather than reinventing the wheel, use a variety of proven information security models, then blend and customize them to fit the needs of your company. In the end, you'll have lots of alternatives to consider. Look at the positive and negative implications of each option. Ultimately, you must decide which end-state vision best fits your current and future needs.

> **Rather than reinventing the wheel, use a variety of proven information security models, then blend and customize them to fit the needs of your company. In the end, you'll have lots of alternatives to consider.**

When you've finished this step, you'll have a high-level view of both the starting and ending points. Both need to be depicted more definitively. The starting point, or current state baseline, consists of the pre-assessment security environment modified by the post-assessment remediation steps. Now, look at the current-state baseline and refine its requirements.

## REFINING THE REQUIREMENTS

Refining the requirements involves taking the current-state baseline and comparing it to current business strategies, then developing a high-level information security strategy and program objectives.

At completion, you will have developed, in addition to the high-level program strategy, a detailed requirements definition for that program, establishing the model for the information security program.

## CREATING A NEW MODEL

Your objective now is to create an information security model based on the high-level strategy and requirements created previously. Then you will blend in best practices, while factoring in present constraints.

Constraints are typically organizational, including culture, resources, management domains, and the like. For example, a corporate culture that leans heavily on open communications and information may balk at changes that entail broader access restrictions. In another instance, a program that includes more stringent and frequent monitoring of network activity logs may be hampered by limited human resources. If the borders separating management domains are either fuzzy or ambiguous, a program that establishes distinct responsibilities will help you avoid confusion, redundant behavior, or an ownership vacuum.

**A corporate culture that leans heavily on open communications and information may balk at changes that entail broader access restrictions.**

Along with the architecture model, you need to thoroughly determine the security risks posed by organizational constraints. Once you've done that, you should organize those risks in terms of priority. Those organizational obstacles that pose the highest risk must be modified or replaced by alternative schemes that either overcome or mitigate those constraints.

You'll also need the cost/benefit analyses for each of the architectural components. Only with a clear understanding of risk potential and mitigation, and the costs and benefits associated with all elements of the model, can you create a program that entails intelligent, high-level, risk management qualities.

## PLANNING THE MIGRATION

By this point, you know where you are, and where you ultimately want to migrate to. Identify all projects that must be completed in order to move from the current environment to the end-state information security environment.

Realistically, there will be different migration plans to consider. They may differ in timing, the number of steps, and the order of steps. You need to understand all the dependencies to be addressed with each migration plan before choosing one of them.

Once you decide, though, you can break the various migration components into more manageable "subprojects" that are easier to scope out in terms of cost, time, and resource requirements.

# AN INTEGRATED ROADMAP TO THE FUTURE

An ESA is an integrated roadmap to the future. It's integrated because it reflects the technology issues you uncovered during your risk assessment, the business drivers elicited from business-unit stakeholders, and the cultural and human resource factors that might confound an otherwise appropriate security architecture.

**By taking a forward-looking, business-driven approach to establishing an ESA, you will be providing a security foundation that can scale and transform with changes to your core business strategies and functions.**

By taking a forward-looking, business-driven approach to establishing an ESA, you will be providing a security foundation that can scale and transform with changes to your core business strategies and functions.

# PART V

# Peering Ahead

# CHAPTER 9

# Taking Back Control

Recently, while commenting on the tense situation in the Middle East, Shimon Peres said that a problem that appears to have no resolution shouldn't be treated as a "problem," it should be treated as a "fact," and dealt with that way. Information risks and security vulnerabilities are not problems. They're facts.

> **Information risks and security vulnerabilities are not problems. They're facts.**

## THE FACTS

According to Forrester Research, U.S. companies with revenues greater than $100 million are spending $213 of every $1 million of revenue on security. That's two-hundredths of one percent of top-line revenue.

Over a 12-month period spanning 1999 and 2000, North American businesses forfeited a total of about 6,822 person-years (defined as one person working a 24-hour-a-day, 365-

day shift) in productivity due to security breaches, down-time, and virus-attack cleanups, according to Reality Research & Consulting.

Worldwide, businesses also experienced about 3.3 percent of unplanned downtime in the last year, which translates to a whopping $1.6 trillion in lost revenue.

These are today's facts; but as we design our response, it's useful to look at what lies ahead. What motives, what opportunities, what opportunists will we face? As we examine some of these, think about how they might be factored into your ESA effort.

## WHO'S MORE MOTIVATED?
## US VERSUS THEM

In October 2000, Simon Singh, the author of the international bestseller, *The Code Book*, issue a code-cracking challenge. The first prize of £10,000 was to be paid to whomever could decipher a set of 10 increasingly difficult codes. The last one was considered the most difficult code ever constructed—it took two years for Singh and a colleague to build it. When it looked like no one could get past the ninth level, Singh prepared to call the contest over and issue a £1,000 prize to the team of contestants that had completed the penultimate stage.

Then, a team of Swedish hackers called to claim the prize. It had taken them the equivalent of 70 computer years to crack the 512-bit code. Singh said the code was equivalent to the most stringent ones used to secure financial services transactions. But how many computer thieves have a team and the resources to break such a code?

This team did the work to win the equivalent of a $15,000 prize, and to win acclaim for itself. If cracking a similar code could put billions of dollars into another team's hands ... well, they have the motive, the means, and the opportunity, don't they?

**If cracking a similar code could put billions of dollars into another team's hands...well, they have the motive, the means, and the opportunity, don't they?**

That is the kind of collaboration that's dangerous. Gartner Group's William Malik agrees. He said, "Posing a far more serious threat [than viruses and script kiddies] are extortionists and embezzlers, who use computers to steal as much as $10 billion per year from the public and private sectors. An even more ominous menace is that presented by impromptu alliances among figures in organized crime, terrorists, and hackers. All three groups have much to gain from collaboration. Their targets will have much to lose, especially as Internet-enabled e-business in government and the private sector becomes routine."

## FIGHTING BACK

As for the rest of us, there's strength in numbers, and that creates very unlikely bedfellows. Imagine IBM, Cisco, Microsoft, and Oracle under the same quilt; that's just where you'll find them. The Information Sharing and Analysis

Center for Information Technology (IT-ISAC) is a nonprofit partnership that teams up government people and others from 19 top high-technology firms, including KPMG. The group's ultimate goal is to respond to computer threats, and it demands that companies that are fiercely competitive collaborate to fight this common threat.

To be sure, IT-ISAC has its work cut out for it. It has to deal with all kinds of attacks—those launched by script kiddies as well as those perpetrated by more stealthy attackers. How the members organize will be driven by how future attacks roll out.

## PEERING AHEAD

Tomorrow's security management challenge will be even more perplexing than today's. Remember those old science fiction stories that made us giggle and shiver in turns with tales of artificially intelligent creatures rising up against their hapless human masters? Remember HAL in *2001: A Space Odyssey?*

While those books and the movie can be safely returned to the entertainment section of your home library, more realistic, though provocative, scenarios do exist.

### Automating the Hack/Counterhack Toolkit

Donn Parker of AtomicTangerine, a venture consulting company, is an expert on computer crime dating back to his career at SRI, and he has a theory about the future: He predicts that hacker tools will become automated. As a result, actual hacking talent itself will become superfluous, and ordinary computer users will be able to perform illegal actions.

In Parker's future, someone could download a program and simply enter in some basic information to trigger a Web crime. The program might prompt the user to enter an amount, say $50,000, and the next day the money would appear in that person's bank account. Meanwhile, half a world away, an accountant would find the books out of balance by the same amount, but the malicious program would leave nary a trace. Parker estimates we could see such crimes begin before 2005.

By the same token, counterhacking techniques will also become automated. Some foresee software robots, or softbots, walking a virtual police beat, performing regular network and perimeter scans on the lookout for unusual activity.

## How Do You Secure Something That's Smarter Than You?

In 1997, it finally happened. A hotly contested competition followed the world over was decided, and in no uncertain terms. But the victor received no flowers, no airy embrace from assembled dignitaries. Instead, someone simply reached over and pressed the Off button. It was Deep Blue, the IBM supercomputer that clobbered grand master Garry Kasparov at chess. That event marked a turning point, the first time a computer had ever outsmarted a human. It also marked one of the first times the world got

**That event marked a turning point, the first time a computer had ever outsmarted a human.**

to see very sophisticated algorithms join with massively powerful processing to address an extremely difficult challenge. In Kasparov's case, Deep Blue used 32 processing engines to contemplate 200 million chess moves each second. Quick thinking, indeed.

Since that event, engineers have gone on to design computers that are a thousand times more powerful than Deep Blue and run a hundred times faster. Last summer, an international team of scientists announced that it had developed the world's first DNA motor. Incredible though it may sound, these motors can be used to develop molecular electronic circuits that are thousands of times faster and smaller than silicon chips.

Hewlett-Packard's Quantum Science Research project has grown "quantum wires" just 10 atoms wide on a silicon surface. These new chips will be exponentially more powerful than the silicon variety, and vastly more efficient to manufacture. They'll also be small enough to fit directly into your body or into tiny medical devices, opening up a huge array of possible applications.

These are fascinating innovations, and the security implications are equally intriguing. When we talked with Craig Mundie, Microsoft's senior vice president of advanced strategies, about these issues, he said he believes that our current computer systems are reaching the limits of their ability to administer information in a secure state.

Think about it: If you networked Deep Blue together with Blue Gene (its younger, more brawny cousin), then

threw in a few molecular computers, you'd have one mighty powerful network. Such supercomputer networks or Super Nets are
already being planned. Often
referred to as grids, the Super
Nets will need the network equivalent of a power utility grid to
support the massive volume of
data being transmitted.

> **Often referred to as grids, the Super Nets will need the network equivalent of a power utility grid to support the massive volume of data being transmitted.**

How do you manage information security in this context? What would happen if a virus spread in this environment? Many supercomputers are being designed with a
much higher degree of fault tolerance. In time, technology
will have to advance to a state such that an infected zone
within a computer can be "locked down" without impairing
the ongoing performance of the rest of the computer.

## Wireless Devices: Securing the Invisible

Today, most security-related discussion tends to focus on
computers, whether they're enclosed within the four walls
of our office place or at home. Less attention is being given
to the growing array of wireless devices in use now or being
developed.

New and futuristic devices will have applications and
implications on a commercial, political, geographical, and
personal level. We've all heard about cell phone technology
that will allow us to order pizza, book flights, send email,

trade stocks, give a precise GPS location, and even act as a TV remote control.

Think about tiny little homing devices that can be attached to your children's clothing to protect them from getting lost or abducted; or biomedical devices that can be implanted to manage cholesterol levels, inject drugs on time release, provide simulated nerve impulses that make prosthetics move like real limbs. "What about in the future when someone has a pacemaker that is controlled by a program that can be modified by a doctor's wireless inputs? Consider the security implications of someone hacking into that system," Craig Mundie of Microsoft suggests.

> "What about in the future when someone has a pacemaker that is controlled by a program that can be modified by a doctor's wireless inputs? Consider the security implications of someone hacking into that system," Craig Mundie, SVP of advanced strategies for Microsoft.

In business, wireless devices will beam on a conference room wall and enable real-time presentations; run quality assurance checks on goods being manufactured; radically alter advertising and brand management by bringing to life, virtually, static logos and ads; and transform order procurement processes and other functions. Similar wireless and satellite technology will increasingly be used to monitor our national defense, capturing data, pictures, and sound to track terrorist groups and spy on hostile governments.

Security around many of these applications is still fairly weak. Cellular phones are a good example. Many of the security risks native to traditional desktop computing transfer easily to those devices. The various cells, networks, and security domains that cell phone users pass through and access provide many opportunities for those with malicious intent. As your phone travels like a relay baton between them, it can be compromised with poisoned downloads; transferred to faulty, fake nodes where data is stolen; tampered with, redirected, and eavesdropped upon; or simply subjected to the same outages and denial of service attacks that cripple desktop computing.

> **The various cells, networks and security domains that cell phone users pass through and access provide many opportunities for those with malicious intent.**

In traditional networks, the would-be attacker is generally obliged to pursue its targets; but in the wireless arena, the switching on and off between cell zones and administrative boundaries makes it conceivably easier for those with illegal motives to act. That's because a malingerer simply needs to wait in any one cell spot while streams of possible targets move unwittingly toward it. The same characteristics that make it easy to lie in wait also make it harder to track down those perpetrators who do so. Malicious users can flick on and off in different cell areas, making them as tricky to catch as a firefly on a summer's night.

## Complexity—Weaving a Tangled Web

The trend-monitoring group, Forecasting International, predicts that by 2005, most companies and government agencies will be using artificial intelligence, data mining, and virtual reality to solve problems beyond the range of today's computers. That may be an optimistic date, but there is no question that, in the future, all devices—computers, wireless or otherwise—will exhibit increasing levels of complexity and sophistication.

"Ultimately," says Microsoft's Mundie, "the task of security will surpass human ability to understand, react, and control it directly. Whereas today our focus is on architecture and programming, tomorrow it will be on policy and administration. And computers will be doing more of the administration, automatically, with little or no human intervention."

That brings up another issue. We are already lacking in people with adequate security talent. That dearth will be exacerbated in the future. New technologies require more highly educated workers with advanced training. The demand for scientists, designers, and engineers, already great, will continue to grow.

A research report by Forecasting International states: "the half-life of an engineer's knowledge today is only five years; in 10 years, 90 percent of what an engineer knows will be available on the computer. In electronics, fully half of what a student learns as a freshman is obsolete by his senior year."

**In electronics, fully half of what a student learns as a freshman is obsolete by his senior year.**

In the situation that is emerging, the likelihood of human error will increase in lockstep with sophisticated advances in technology. The response should be more people, better education, and frequent training. But what we, in fact, have is fewer people, moderate education, and infrequent training. The solution, Mundie believes, is that "computers will become the detail-level administrators, implementing network and security policies, themselves."

This isn't a big conceptual stretch, either. In the case of Kasparov and the computer, those chess algorithms were the genius of the programmers; implementing those chess "policies" was the computer's job. Will human genius always drive the process, no matter how intelligent machines ultimately become? And as our role moves up the levels of abstraction and machines take on more and more of the lower-level details, how does this effect the scope of our control?

What does this do to the audit role? Today, humans control the audit, so if a mistake is made, you can go to the humans in question and talk it out. Imagine if computers controlled the audit. Who would have overall responsibility? Would we even know there was a problem? Could we end up in an Arthur C. Clarke world where the computers outsmart us and work behind our backs?

**Imagine if computers controlled the audit. Who would have overall responsibility? Would we even know there was a problem?**

These issues will continue to foment rich discussion and experimentation among scientists, engineers, and academics for some time to come. For now, however, let's turn our attention back to the less sci-fi present.

## POWERLESS OR POWERFUL

At this point, no one would blame you if you felt powerless to prevent attacks to your network, or paranoid about insider threats. From one perspective the situation appears totally out of your control. But it isn't. You do have some control.

Every time you get in your car and drive out of your driveway, you assume some risk, and that risk is constantly shifting. On local streets, on a weekday at noon, there are different levels of risk than when you enter that highway on-ramp soon after. We're not sure what all the different levels are; we just know they're there.

Many of those risks are ones you have no control over. You can't control the driving skills of the person in the car behind or in front of you. You can't control the condition of the road—the oil slicks, the potholes. Does that mean you're at the mercy of these factors? Not at all. You can manage your risk by making sure your tires have sufficient tread, your brakes are working properly, and you are driving sensibly. As a result, even though you and the driver next to you are driving on the same road at the same time, your risks may be very different.

The same holds true for the Internet and e-businesses. Yes, all Web sites and their associated enterprises share this same stretch of highway. All face the same set of factors that are beyond their control. But their risks are different.

Have Microsoft's or Yahoo!'s or Bank of America's executive team assessed its information risks? Have they concluded that the frequency of intrusions is consistent with the value of the assets that are exposed, the vulnerabilities they have, and the threats they face? If so, then we'd say they are managing those risks.

Is your company looking at the whole picture? Are you factoring in both the opportunities and the risks in making decisions about your security environment? Is your security environment complementary to your business practices, or is it bolted on and creating drag?

> **Is your security environment complementary to your business practices, or is it bolted on and creating drag?**

A company that has not been successfully attacked but believes security is a technology problem and foists it off onto an IT manager is simply lucky. That's all. And that luck will change.

A company—even one that has been successfully attacked—that has established an appropriate security environment, one that can change with the changes in business and risk, is in control. That company will not depend upon luck to protect its reputation, its assets, and its customers' trust. That's taking control.

# CHAPTER 10

# Privacy and Security

IBM recently created a new position—chief privacy officer. The U.S. Defense Department has given the green light to active network intrusion countermeasures, essentially permitting the military to take off its gloves when responding to intrusions.

IBM's action certainly signals its attention to what is a growing national—and global—concern. The Defense Department's position reflects how seriously it views intrusions of military networks. Privacy and security: Is this a case of synergy, or parallel play?

**Privacy and security: Is this a case of synergy, or parallel play?**

There are those who would lump privacy and security together, maintaining that you can't have one without the other. But are the two inexorably linked? Whereas we certainly see their interrelationship, we are not so sure the two must be treated as parts of an indivisible whole.

For example, one could devise a security architecture that prevents most penetrations, detects those few exceptions, and responds to intrusions quickly and definitively. That security environment would address the physical and cyberspace realms within which the company does business. It could be refined to do an appropriate job of keeping external attackers at bay, while appropriately managing internal information security risks. At the same time, though, that company could also be selling its customer information lists —lists that have been gathered through a very secure infrastructure—to others, unbeknownst to its customers.

You could argue that the company is doing a great security job, but most customers would agree that its privacy score is abominable. In other words, a company could have appropriate information security coupled with an objectionable use of personal information. The two are not naturally coupled.

On the other hand, if a company's privacy policy is to keep all personal information unshared, but its security architecture is so woefully lacking that outsiders were able to access clear-text customer records, then that company is both a security and privacy failure. In this case, its privacy failure is unwitting, but ignorance, as we all know, is no defense.

Security is an issue that goes well beyond technology, and privacy is an issue that goes well beyond security. Privacy goes to the ethical heart of a business, and has much less to do with how the information is collected than with how the information is to be used.

> **Security is an issue that goes well beyond technology. Privacy is an issue that goes well beyond security.**

Michael Capellas, CEO of Compaq Computer, put it this way: "I believe the issue of privacy is a far larger issue [than security]. We will be able to get highly secure transactions over the Web. This is a short-term problem. It takes a little time to optimize it. Privacy is a more complex and difficult question. It crosses social boundaries; it's a philosophical and strategic issue."

With regard to the possible roles of government and industry in resolving the privacy issue, Capellas sees a joint role for each. "It needs to be a combination of the federal government and business. Government can set a general baseline; industry can make it happen. The government must take a role in awareness and in setting the agenda for public policy forums. In fact, the government can force collaboration and even go so far as to issue guidelines. But after establishing the guidelines, the solution has to be turned over to the private sector in order to make it happen, technologically."

The U.S. government appears to be chomping at the bit to get privacy legislation in motion. The essence of some proposed pieces of legislation is for a company to assume that it has no permission to share personal data unless the individual "opts in," or gives consent. This is already the regulatory position governing information use adopted by the European Union, for example. In the U.S., though, many companies offer an "opt out" choice. They tell you what they routinely do with your information, and give you the choice of saying "no."

**In privacy matters, should we assume something is forbidden unless it is expressly permitted, or assume something is permitted unless it is expressly forbidden.**

In privacy matters, should we assume something is forbidden unless it is expressly permitted, or assume something is permitted unless it is expressly forbidden?

It wasn't long ago that local phone companies were pushing caller ID. People who had that service would be able to see the source telephone numbers of incoming calls. The idea was to enable users to decide whether to answer a call or not. That's personalization, right? But if you called a tire company to inquire about prices, they also saw your number, and could presumably follow up with unsolicited telemarketing calls. Most people in California were opposed to caller ID. Yet Pacific Bell made it an opt-out rather than an opt-in feature. Consumers were not pleased.

On the other hand, Web sites such as Amazon.com use cookies (snippets of code related to previous visits and activity) and other ordering information to gain insight into your choice of books. Each time you visit the site, after having bought a book on, say, Internet Security, you'll be greeted with suggestions of other titles of interest. It is done in an inoffensive way, and your information isn't shared outside of Amazon. Cheaptickets.com also keeps track of who you are and what you've purchased. In fact, if you disable the cookie feature on your browser (which you can do), you cannot transact with them.

Perhaps instead of taking pre-cipitous action, there needs to be more of an airing of public opin-ion. George ("Jay") Keyworth, chairman of the Progress &

**Perhaps instead of taking precipitous action, there needs to be more of an airing of public opinion.**

Freedom Foundation and member of the board of directors of Hewlett-Packard, has his opt-in reservations. "My con-cern is that, of course, the government will always attempt to take preemptive action before the data are in. No one dis-putes the American peoples' concern over privacy. It's part of our fabric. But how do we manage it? We need to know what people really value. We were telling people what was important when we should have been listening. We need to be very careful; opt-in is too big a step."

Keyworth, who was a science advisor to former Presi-dent Reagan, says his firsthand experiences in Washington, D.C. provide additional shading to his opinion. "Govern-ment does have a right to act. But right now 'opt-in' puts government in the leading role to make that decision. I think it's plain wrong and naïve."

But privacy is an issue that attracts the public's attention. Then President Clinton, speaking in May 2000 at a com-mencement at Eastern Michigan University, said, "The same technology that links distant places can also be used to track our every move online. In this information age we can't let new opportunities erode old fundamental rights. We can't let breakthroughs in technology break down laws of priva-cy." And Senator Ernest Hollings (D-South Carolina) said at a recent Congressional hearing, "Any bill that doesn't have 'opt-in' is just whistling Dixie."

The 107th Congress faces a whopping 48 privacy bills in 2001. All of the bills, either in whole or in part, focus on privacy regimes, practices, or protections, or otherwise contain direct references to privacy laws and definitions. At least eight of them are directly tied to technology.

**The 107th Congress is facing a whopping 48 privacy bills this year.**

They include:

- ❏ The Electronic Privacy Protection Act.
- ❏ The Spyware Control and Privacy Protection Act (sounds like it's right out of a James Bond flick).
- ❏ The Online Privacy Protection Act.
- ❏ The Unsolicited Commercial Electronic Mail Act.
- ❏ The Consumer Internet Privacy Enhancement Act.
- ❏ The Consumer Online Privacy and Disclosure Act.
- ❏ The Social Security On-line Privacy Protection Act.
- ❏ The Internet Tax Nondiscrimination Act.

While the House and Senate stand divided more often than not, the subject of privacy finds members of both sides of the aisle converging. If bipartisan support grows, some form of privacy legislation may be enacted soon.

**Privacy is not solely a risk issue, nor is it only an operational issue. It has become a strategic business issue that is holistic.**

Privacy is not solely a risk issue, nor is it only an operational issue. It has become a strategic business issue that is holistic, and one that needs to be applied enterprisewide. If you do it right, the impact on customer trust can be enormous, and trust is ultimately the catalyst for trade.

## PRIVACY AND YOUR ESA

Whether or not the government passes privacy regulation any time soon, pursue your ESA efforts now. In the absence of clear privacy rules, each company's privacy ethics should prevail. Typically these privacy needs will have less to do with how you transact business and collect information than with who has access to it and what they do with it. So, while legislation will affect your ESA over time, an appropriately structured ESA should be able to accommodate those changes in a nondisruptive way.

For example, if pending privacy legislation is passed and it affects the way you are currently handling information, you should be able to accommodate those changes through modifications of policies and procedures, without having to make wholesale changes to underlying technologies.

## SECURITY IS NOW

Regulations regarding the privacy of information gathered online or the taxation of goods and services sold online are still fodder for a round of heated polemics. But DoS attacks, network intrusions, and other forms of network high jinks are real. Don't wait for the resolution of privacy and other regulatory matters before developing and implementing your ESA. Attackers, whether inside or outside, aren't waiting either. You owe it to your stockholders, customers, partners, and employees to make investing in you, buying from you, teaming with you, and working for you a safe, secure, and reliable experience.

# Bibliography

Cetron, Marvin J. and Davies, Owen. "Trends Now Changing the World: Technology, the Workplace, Management, and Institutions." *The Futurist*, 2, 35, p. 27.

Computer Security Alert, Computer Security Institute, San Francisco, CA.

Giussani, Bruno. "The World Economic Forum's Big Hack Attack." *The Standard*, February 4, 2001.

Harrison, Ann. "Teens Crack PacBell ISP." *Computerworld*, January 17, 2000, p.16.

Hess, Pamela. "Pentagon OKs Experimental Tech Projects." UPI, February 2, 2001.

Hu, Jim. "MTV 'Hack' Backfires." CNET News.com, September 9, 1998.

"Intrusion-Detection Services ... Damaging." *Informationweek*, May 29, 2000.

Landers, Jim. "Experts Caution of Internet Weakness." *The Dallas Morning News*, January 30, 2001.

Loeb, Vernon. "Launching a Counteroffensive ... Security." *Washington Post*, February 5, 2000, p. A3.

Lytle, Tamara. "NASA Computers Easily Penetrated." *Austin American-Statesman*, May 22, 1999.

"Media Examples of Security Breaches." ADD Secure.Net.

Merkow, Mark S. and Breithaupt, James. *The Complete Guide to Internet Security*. New York: AMACOM, 2000.

Noack, David. "The Top 10 Computer Security Flaws." APB News.com, June 2, 2000.

Ptacek, Thomas and Newsham, Timothy. "Insertion, Evasion, and Denial of Service ... Detection." Secure Networks Inc., January, 1998.

Schneier, Bruce. *Secrets & Lies: Digital Security in a Networked World*. New York: John Wiley & Sons, 2000.

Shipley, Greg. "How Secure Is Your Network?" *Network Computing*, November 27, 2000.

Smith, Greg. "Nab 3 in Sprint Cyberscam." *Daily News* (New York), January 14, 2000.

Smith, Homer Wilson. *Lessons from a Security Breach*. Security Breach Lessons.

Zakaria, Tabassuj. "CIA Secret Chat Room Investigated." Reuters, November 12, 2000.

# Glossary

**Algorithm**  A precise set of rules specifying how to solve complex mathematical problems.

**Application Service Provider (ASP)**  A company that hosts software applications on its own servers within its own facilities for other companies.

**Asynchronous Transfer Mode (ATM)**  A network technology for both LANs and WANs that supports real-time voice and video as well as data.

**Authentication**  Any system by which a system attempts to validate that users are, in fact, who they claim to be.

**BIND (Berkeley Internet Name Domain)**  A public domain DNS server that is available for most versions of UNIX.

**Biometrics**  An identification process that includes eyes, voice, handprints, fingerprints, and handwritten signatures.

**Checksum**  A numeric value that is calculated based on the specific characters and their positions in every line of a program. A change in a single character, or spacing, will produce a markedly different checksum; so these values are fast ways of determining if anything about a program has been changed.

**Computer Emergency Response Team (CERT)**  Started in December 1988 by the Defense Advanced Research Projects Agency (DARPA), which was part of the U.S. Department of Defense; a federally funded research center operated by Carnegie Mellon University.

**Cookies** Code used to identify a user to a Web site, possibly for the purpose of delivering customized Web pages to that user.

**Cracker** Someone who breaks into a computer system without authorization and whose purpose is to do damage. Often used interchangeably with "hacker."

**Cryptography** The study of codes; refers to the making and breaking of algorithms to conceal or otherwise encrypt information.

**DDoS (Distributed Denial of Service)** A type of denial-of-service attack that co-opts thousands of computer systems with the purpose of generating a broad-based simultaneous attack on a Web site.

**Decryption** The process of decoding data that has been encrypted into a secret format.

**Default configuration** The original system setting.

**Demilitarized zone (DMZ)** A subnet that contains a firewall and proxy server; serves as a divider between a company's intranet and the Web.

**Digital exchange** An online marketplace of suppliers, vendors, and customers.

**Directory** The Unix equivalent of a Macintosh or MS-Windows "folder," all files are stored in directories.

**Domain** A subsection of the Internet such as .com, .net, and .org. These domains are administered by the InterNIC.

**Domain Name Server (DNS)** An Internet service that translates domain names into IP addresses.

**DoS (Denial of Service)** A state in which a system can no longer respond to normal requests. An attack on a network that inundates it with so many additional requests that regular traffic is either slowed or completely interrupted.

**ECHO** To transmit received data back to the sending station, allowing the user to visually inspect what was received.

**EDI (Electronic Data Interchange)** The electronic communication of business transactions between organizations.

**Encryption** The process of using cryptography to protect data from unauthorized access.

**Enterprise Resource Planning (ERP)** A business management system that integrates all facets of the business, including planning, manufacturing, sales, and marketing.

**Enterprise Security Architecture (ESA)** An enterprise-wide framework for managing security risks.

**Ethernet** A LAN protocol developed by Xerox Corporation in cooperation with DEC and Intel in 1976. Supports data transfer rates of 10 Mbps. One of the most widely implemented LAN standards.

**Exploit** A software program designed to take advantage of a known system vulnerability.

**File Transfer Protocol (FTP)** A communications protocol used to transmit files without loss of data. A protocol used to transfer files over a TCP/IP network.

**Firewall** A system designed to prevent unauthorized access to or from a private network.

**Grep (Global-Regular-Expression-Print)** A utility that allows you to search through files for specific patterns.

**Hacker** Once a slang term for a computer enthusiast, now more commonly interchanged with "cracker" to refer to individuals who access computer networks for the purpose of stealing and corrupting data.

**http (Hyper Text Transport Protocol)** The system for requesting HTML (Hyper Text Markup Language) documents from the Web.

**ICMP (Internet Control Message Protocol)** An extension to the Internet Protocol (IP); the standard error and control message protocol for Internet systems.

**Internet protocol (IP)** Refers to all the standards that keep the Internet running. The foundation protocol is TCP/IP, which provides the basic communications mechanism as well as ways to copy files and send e-mail.

**Internet protocol (IP) address**  The specific address of a computer attached to a TCP/IP network.

**Internet Service Provider (ISP)**  A company that provides access to the Internet.

**InterNIC database**  A database containing information related to domain-name registration.

**IPX packets (Internetwork Packet Exchange)**  A protocol used for connectionless communications.

**Neutrality seal**  Certifies that an exchange or enterprise has satisfied a strict list of criteria and gives users a strong measure of comfort that the exchange is acting in a totally neutral, unbiased fashion.

**Null password**  A setting in which no password has been selected and anyone can gain access.

**Operating system (OS)**  The master control program that runs the computer.

**Packet**  In network communications, a combination of a "header" with identifying information and a "body" containing the data to be transmitted.

**Password**  A word or code used to serve as a security measure against unauthorized access to data.

**Ping (Packet Internet Groper)**  A utility to determine whether a specific IP address is live and reachable.

**Proxy server**  Used for host servers behind firewalls. The proxy server intercepts and relays all requests to the real server.

**Public Key Infrastructure (PKI)**  A system of digital certificates to authenticate and identify the various parties of an Internet message or transaction.

**Root access**  Allows users to access all files at all levels. The highest degree of system access.

**Rootkit**  A hacker toolset used for accumulating passwords.

**Router**  A special type of Internet host that transfers packets between two or more networks.

**Script kiddie** An unsophisticated hacker wannabee, who explores network systems looking for known vulnerabilities without really understanding much about them.

**Secure Sockets Layer (SSL)** Developed by Netscape, the leading security mechanism on the Internet. When an SSL session is started, the server sends its public key to the browser, which the browser uses to send a randomly generated secret key back to the server in order to have a secret key exchange for that session.

**Service Advertising Protocol (SAP)** A NetWare protocol used to identify the services and addresses of servers attached to the network.

**Simple Network Management Protocol (SNMP)** A set of protocols for managing complex networks. SNMP works by sending messages to different parts of a network.

**SMTP (Simple Mail Transfer Protocol)** A protocol for sending e-mail messages between servers.

**Smurf** A type of denial-of-service attack. An attack on a network that floods it with excessive messages in order to hinder normal traffic and eventually cause an overload.

**Sniffer** A program and/or device that monitors data traveling over a network. Sniffers can be used both for legitimate network management functions and for stealing information from a network. Unauthorized sniffers can be extremely dangerous to a network's security because they are virtually impossible to detect and can be inserted almost anywhere. This makes them a favorite weapon in the hacker's arsenal.

**Social engineering** The ability of a hacker to break into a system simply by fooling an employee into revealing access codes, passwords, and other confidential information.

**Spoof** To replace a correct Web address with a phony one.

**SYN flood attack** An assault on a network that prevents a TCP/IP server from servicing other users.

**System Integration Controls (SIC)** Verification tools for companies to check that optimal systems controls relating to a major application implementation are in place and operating effectively.

**TCP/IP (Transmission Control Protocol/Internet Protocol)** A communications protocol developed under contract from the U.S. Department of Defense to internetwork dissimilar systems.

**Token Ring** The PC network protocol developed by IBM.

**Trojan programs** Innocuous-looking programs that purport to do one thing but actually do something else.

**UTC** The international time standard (formerly Greenwich Mean Time, or GMT). Zero hours UTC is midnight in Greenwich, England.

**VPN (Virtual Private Network)** A private network that is configured within a public network. VPNs have the security of a private network from access control and encryption, while taking advantage of large public networks.

# New Strategies for Success in E-Business

## Managing Risks to Protect Brand, Retain Customers, and Enhance Market Capitalization

## INTRODUCTION

As e-business evolves, it continues to change "the shape of enterprise, the speed of action, the nature of leadership,"[1] along with the risks and opportunities all organizations face. Whether they are traditional companies or pure dot-com enterprises—or any iteration along the digitization continuum—all organizations will become subject to the evolving rules of the new economy.

As leaders develop strategies for operating in this new environment, they recognize that their critical challenges are few but fundamental. To be successful, an e-business strategy must enable an organization to:

---

Excerpted from the KPMG White Paper, "New Strategies for Success in E -Business: Managing Risks to Protect Brand, Retain Customers, and Enhance Market Capitalization," written and prepared by KPMG's Information Risk Management Practice and Assurance and Advisory Services Center, KPMG, 2001.

❏ Protect brand,

❏ Optimize shareholder value, and

❏ Maximize opportunities for enhancing revenues and reducing costs.

Experience shows that failure in any of these areas will ultimately erode shareholder and consumer confidence. Customer service failures, especially, are exacerbated in a "24/7" e-business setting, where mistakes or weak spots can soon become common knowledge, causing harm to the organization's brand, reputation, and market value. Such failures are exponentially harmful in an environment characterized by ongoing change in processes, expectations, and competitors—and continually subject to attack.

In fact, attacks and other technology failures are an inevitable part of an e-business commitment. Consequently, "As enterprises move more revenue into e-business channels, information-security risk increases."[2] Risk management in an e-business environment is of primary concern to corporate directors, who indicated as much in a recent KPMG survey. These leaders realize that the interconnectivity now enabling business means that organizations no longer function as entirely discrete entities. Moreover, business relationships are now by nature digitally "invasive"—and thus, reliant on a variety of new information flows enabled by technology. As a result, because "commodifying relationships ... [is] the essential business of business,"[3] the organization that can best assure its customers and e-business partners of information security, privacy, high availability, and access will create a new competitive advantage.

In an effort to create that e-business advantage, many leaders are asking fundamental questions, including:

❏ How does digitization affect our business risks?

❏ Have we identified the right business model?

❏ Can we identify our digital category, and how will we move into our optimal e-space? (See Figure 1.)

| Description | Traditional Enterprise | Transitional Enterprise | Digitized Enterprise | Digital Enterprise | Pure Dot-com Enterprise |
|---|---|---|---|---|---|
| **Product** | Tangible, not digitizable products | Tangible products, offered through traditional channels | Tangible products, offered both traditionally and digitally | Principally digital or digitizable products | All digital products |
| **Processes** | Traditional processes with classic technology controls | Transitional, technology-applied production processes | High-technology processes digitally managed, with a strong movement toward "webification" | Principally digital processes, digitally controlled | All digital processes |
| **Degree of e-integration into traditional products and services** | Limited | Under design to expand | Selectively integrated internally; just started externally | Internally strong; digitally integrated with suppliers and customers; strong digital partnerships | Highly connected externally, but value diffused |
| **Business model** | Traditional business model | Seeking new business model | Blended business model | New-economy business model | Internet-digital business model |

*Figure 1   How Organizations Define and Occupy an e-Space (Source: KPMG 2001)*

❏ Have we properly aligned our controls, systems, investments, and business and information strategies?

❏ Can we continue to adapt?

Once they have an e-business strategy in place, they can begin to align that strategy with risk management. To meet and exceed the expectations of e-business customers and business partners, organizations need to then consider whether they have ensured the security, accuracy, completeness, and integrity of information assets. Just as important, they need to determine whether they have ensured the reliability of e-business processes and their ability to execute transactions at any time. The answers to these questions will become the foundation of an e-business risk-management framework (encompassing information security, business continuity, applications systems, and infrastructure controls)—a framework that is a fundamental strategic component of any sustainable e-business endeavor.

Rather than functioning as a drag on organizational innovation, an e-business risk-management framework is an e-business enabler. It is tied to issues such as:

❏ Are we taking sufficient risk?

❏ Does our organizational culture support and extend our e-business initiatives?

❏ Do we have the right relationships in place? Which vendors and partners should we be allied with, now and in the future?

❏ How is our competitive landscape evolving?

❏ Are our investments appropriate?

❏ Are our people the best ones for the job at hand, and are they in the right positions?

❏ Have we given our employees the responsibility for specific aspects of risk management and the authority to act on that responsibility?

❑ Does our staff take proper precautions for conducting business online? Are guidelines for such behavior widely communicated?

❑ How do we know that our systems will always be available?

❑ How quickly could we react if they were not available?

❑ What is the cost of a virus attack, and what should we spend to prevent it?

An organization should design a risk-management framework that reflects its overall strategic intent as well as its new e-risks. This strategic imperative calls for a comprehensive yet rapid approach to risk-management design and deployment. The organization should focus on optimizing its current risks as well as those in the e-space it wants to occupy (see Figure 1), beginning with the strategy it intends to deploy to get there and with an awareness of the new risks it will face along the way.

## USING RISK MANAGEMENT TO ENABLE E-BUSINESS

In the rush to develop an e-business presence, many organizations arrive at the electronic marketplace poorly prepared, perhaps with only a vague understanding of the nature of the new risks they face and how to identify, mitigate, and optimize them. As a result, their mistakes and other challenges result from poor business practices, which are supported, at best, by inadequate controls.

Risk management is by no means a simple technology issue, just as the risks related to control failures are not simply technology risks (see Figure 2). Organizational culture, for example, is one of the most basic, most critical, and most overlooked aspects of e-business security. Ethical standards—articulated by the board and upheld by management—are vital to success in an e-business environment, in which organizations are increasingly connected to, and reliant on, individuals and systems they do not directly over-see. e-Business risk management must address the cultural issues inherent in deploying an effective e-business strategy.

Operational success also demands strong risk management and a risk-management-conscious culture. In many organizations, for example, operations employees do not understand the business impact of the risks associated with their decisions (and, conversely, many executives do not understand the operational effects of their decisions). Consequently even simple risk-management efforts—such as enhancing the security of a Web domain—are often overlooked. Such oversights can lead to Web site hijackings, which expose the organization to the risk of reputation damage or loss of intellectual property. The impact of e-business is such that a single failure can dry up an organization's revenue stream and drive off customers—whereas in the not-too-distant past, technology failures tended to affect only single locations or back-end processes. As part of its risk-management framework, organizations also need diagnostic controls to help them assess and investigate problems, as well as interactive controls, which can help them respond to marketplace developments. They also need a means of knowing when they are being attacked, and a plan that dictates what to do when (not if) it happens.

As described in the following sections, an e-business strategy, implementation, and operations scenario must be aligned with the goals of the overall business so that a risk-management framework can be designed and deployed to enable the e-business to move quickly and decisively.

Figure 2 depicts the six areas in which the organization should define business risks and link them to e-business risk management. The bottom line: risk management should be integrated at the outset, not bolted on at the end.

*In managing for e-business risks, most organizations focus on specific applications or technology solutions (such as SAP security or imple-*

| Aspects of a Risk-Management Framework | Vision | Potential Risks of Failure |
| --- | --- | --- |
| Strategy | Business, e-business, IT, and risk-management strategies are defined, aligned, and supported by all levels of management, and they are communicated enterprise-wide | Brand and channel conflict; failed initiatives |
| e-Business Risk and Program Management | The structure, resources, and skills needed to execute the risk-management strategy are defined and in place | Inability to plan for and react to events; inability to develop and support e-business initiatives |
| Policies and Procedures | Policies, procedures, and guidelines are developed, implemented, and communicated, and they effectively support the risk-management strategy | Front-line staff operate in a manner that is out of sync with the business strategy |
| Operations and Monitoring | Processes are in place to effectively implement, maintain, and monitor the policies, procedures, and service-level objectives | Warnings are missed, and avoidable problems are realized |
| Applications Infrastructure | Applications and related processes support transaction and data integrity, confidentiality, and availability | Inefficient business processes; exposures and fraud |
| Technology Infrastructure | A strategically designed technical infrastructure is designed and in place; it includes hardware, software, communications, middleware, and other enabling technologies that are ubiquitous, available, secure, reliable, scalable, and flexible | Revenue stream break; systems failures |

*Figure 2   A Model for e-Business Risk Management*

*menting firewalls). But the risk-management focus should begin with strategy, and it should seek to address the risks inherent in each layer of the model. Failure to do so can create unnecessary risks that could affect the revenue stream and, thereby, the organization's brand, customer retention, and market capitalization.*

## 1. Strategy

Accustomed to success in their existing business models, organizations may not have considered how they will define and measure success in an e-business model. "Even where e-business seems an obvious fit, its adoption will require changes in technology, processes, and people."[4] An organization must determine its vision and goals for the e-business, identify the e-business drivers, and then develop plans and strategies to achieve the goals within the defined context of the business drivers. Then, to ensure that e-risk management reflects and supports their overall objectives, leaders must align their e-business strategy with their overall strategies for the business, its information technology, and risk management. One of the most significant risks an organization faces is the consistent integration of these endeavors, which must be linked and supported by management across the enterprise, beginning at the CEO and board levels.

Most organizations pursue e-business along multiple channels (B2B, B2C, B2M, internal, and others). A risk-management framework must consider these dimensions and how they could affect customers, suppliers, and employees. Considerations will include:

❑ What are the intended benefits of e-business for the organization, and what might its key performance indicators encompass?

❑ How will industry trends and competitor efforts influence the marketplace and the organization's e-business pursuits?

❑ How will potential mergers or acquisitions affect the e-business strategy and the resulting organizational business model?

## 1. Strategy

### Key Strategic Risks in Defining and Occupying an e-Space

Examples of strategic e-business risks to be considered at either the organizational, functional, and/or business unit level include:

- Consistency of the e-business strategy with the overall business strategy
- Failure to understand what the customer/market wants (or is prepared for)
- Impact that strategic decisions will have on people, processes, or technology
- Failure to understand the current and future capabilities of the technology
- Incomplete or inaccurate data (historical and current performance, market size, and expectations)
- Impact of existing or proposed legislation or regulation
- Failure to take advantage of alliances with key partners
- Failure to understand new and existing competitor activity
- Failure to protect privacy
- Failure to use data as an asset to develop new markets

*Figure 3*

❏ Have we identified "boundary controls" that will guide our people ethically yet not stifle their ability to innovate?

❏ How can e-business risks be identified, mitigated, and optimized with a comprehensive system of internal controls?

Part of this process is to determine how to use e-business strategically so that the organization can define and occupy an e-space in a way that best suits its culture and its customers. Organizations should ensure that all channels are integrated and operate to create seamless customer experiences. The specifics of the strategy will, in turn, determine the nature and scope of the risk management framework that is designed and implemented to support it.

Development of an e-business strategy carries with it the risks that the strategic aims are sub-optimal, the market and other data on which it is based are incomplete or inaccurate, opportunities will be missed, and unforeseen issues (such as competitive threats)

**Key Considerations and Strategies at the Strategy Level**

| Considerations | Potential Strategies |
|---|---|
| · Who should have access to organizational assets? | · Ensure that each application has a defined owner who is responsible for access to it |
| · How can the e-business assure availability, reliability, and recovery? | · Create business continuity and high-availability plans<br>· Create capacity plans that reflect predictions of future volume |
| · Which trusted third parties can have what level of access to our internal systems? | · Ensure that operational processes reflect senior management requirements/decisions |
| · To what extent do we need to verify the authenticity of third parties? | · Determine appropriate security architecture, including, for example, a PKI implementation |

*Figure 4*

will arise. Implementation of the strategy could be affected by poor communication of it, lack of resources, inappropriate resources, or lack of operational capability. e-Risk management measures at the strategy level can help address these issues.

Once the organization has developed an e-business strategy and identified the risks it faces in pursuing it, it can begin to create effective internal risk-management measures and develop capabilities (applications systems, information security, business continuity, and infrastructure) focused on the highest risk areas. The risk-management infrastructure must become a formalized, executive-level commitment, with the resources and budget necessary to fulfill its purpose.

## 2. Risk Management Program Development

Once an organization has a macro strategy, it must assign responsibility and authority for implementing and monitoring it. To that end, it should designate a program "office"—even if that office consists of one person—charged with overseeing, directing, and driving the implementation of the e-business risk-management initiatives, including interacting with the organization's various network partners and processes. This authority must have the endorsement and support of the highest levels of management

**2. Risk Management Program Development**

*Key Considerations and Strategies at the Program Level*

| Considerations | Potential Strategies |
|---|---|
| • How do we manage security, and is it adequate? | • Establish a security management function that keeps the executive level informed of security status |
| • How do we deal with business continuity issues and internal controls? | • Establish a business continuity management function and an internal audit function |
| • How does the program ensure the integration of multiple systems across entities? | • Establish consistent guidelines for systems integration |

*Figure 5*

and other influential stakeholders. It should be at the heart of a movement to ensure that risk management is not perceived as a "bolt-on" or a necessary evil, but is instead integral to the success of the entire e-business.

The program office will likely:

❏ Operationalize the e-business mission and vision by establishing objectives and metrics for that business
❏ Ensure that the organization's culture accommodates and supports the e-business
❏ Establish an organizational structure as well as roles and responsibilities for carrying out the program
❏ Create processes for hiring appropriately skilled personnel and providing them with training
❏ Establish budget processes and monitor those plans
❏ Define an application development life cycle
❏ Create formal processes for managing legal, regulatory, contractual, and competitive risks

## 3. Policies and Procedures

An organization may have an e-risk management architecture, but no formal framework or documents for implementing it. That

### 3. Policies and Procedures

*Key Considerations and Strategies at the Policies and Procedures Level*

| Considerations | Potential Strategies |
|---|---|
| How do we ensure that our policies are up-to-date and relevant? | Review and update user awareness programs and policies on a regular basis |
| Are controls consistent, with strong links to business drivers and operational processes? | Ensure that line management periodically makes internal audit and other staff aware of key controls in the business processes |
| Does the use of non-standard architecture impede the rollout of central applications and the integration of components? | Ensure that technology standards and purchasing policies exist and are appropriate |
| Do policies and procedures address services provided by third parties? | Establish appropriate service-level agreements, consistent communications, and dedicated resources that know your operations |
| Is the outsourced infrastructure subject to adequate scrutiny? | Review service-level agreements, contracts, and third-party assessments |

*Figure 6*

deficiency has huge implications, for both risk mitigation and market perception. Organizations need to define specific policies and procedures that relate to business strategy, e-strategy, and IT strategy—with a focus on specific risks. These policies must address the organization's diverse array of business processes, technologies, and security and privacy requirements, and they need to be communicated and endorsed at all levels.

## 4. Operations and Monitoring

Once an organization develops policies and procedures for its e-business and related risk management efforts, it must create business processes and operations as well as a method of monitoring them. Many times, organizations will develop security policies and/or procedures, but then fail to institutionalize them with user awareness programs, training, and measurement. Confusion develops, and the policies and procedures become "shelfware" and are ignored. As application architectures are defined and processes change, the organization needs to ensure that every level ties back to the dictates of the program office and undergoes monitoring. Roles and responsibilities for responding to unscheduled disruptions, denial-of-service attacks, viruses, and other intrusions should be an explicit part of this endeavor.

Operations and monitoring efforts can encompass:

❏ Skill levels of IT personnel
❏ Segregation of sensitive positions such as development, production control, database administration, and security
❏ Performance against budget
❏ Financial support levels for e-business initiatives
❏ Service-level definition and agreements with internal customers, third-party service providers, business partners, and external customers
❏ Incident response, including service-level agreements, security, intrusion detection, and component failure

**4. Operations and Monitoring**

*Key Considerations and Strategies at the Operations Level*

| Considerations | Potential Strategies |
| --- | --- |
| Does the organization know and react when intrusions occur? | Assure that plans are in place for monitoring and reporting security breaches |
| | Develop a system for reporting to business units and corporate offices |
| Can the organization recognize and react to unusual events? | Ensure that formal incident-response and escalation procedures are in place and communicated |
| To what extent is the business designed to prevent service interruptions? | Ensure that applications are robust and a tested recovery plan is in place |
| What assurance does the organization have that controls are operating and are effective? | Establish risk-management reviews and quality procedures |
| | Analyze help-desk feedback |
| Is the infrastructure supporting today's, and capable of supporting tomorrow's, transaction volumes? | Perform capacity planning and monitor performance metrics |

*Figure 7*

- ❏ Day-to-day operations
- ❏ Help desk and self-help efforts
- ❏ Customer satisfaction
- ❏ Configuration management and change control procedures
- ❏ Security awareness and training
- ❏ Business continuity and disaster recovery maintenance and operations
- ❏ Use of directory services

## 5. Applications Infrastructure

Most organizations address e-business risk management at the applications level, and then create functional and integrity controls that are divorced from their overall business strategies. In embracing the use of an extranet, for example, organizations make their systems vulnerable to the supply chain. Security measures are often inconsistent from application to application. As large organizations "e-ify," often no common approaches are developed and constant reinvention is necessary, resulting not only in inefficiencies but increased vulnerabilities as well.

**5. Applications Infrastructure**

*Key Considerations and Strategies at the Application Level*

| Considerations | Potential Strategies |
|---|---|
| How is access to critical data managed? | Application security administrators should ensure that data owners understand data access rules |
| Which application should be recovered first? | Ensure that the business impact assessment includes specific applications and business processes |
| Are financial transactions conducted properly? | Perform automated reconciliations, record counts, and control totals |
| Do multiple platforms and technologies mean that application development is difficult, unwieldy, or slow? | Use a standard environment, tools, and middleware to integrate systems |
| What is the impact of changing parts of applications? | Implement organization-wide processes for managing and controlling application changes |

*Figure 8*

Organizations must ensure that their applications have risk-management measures in place that are commensurate with the business risks related to processes, security, and interfaces. They must also ensure that the applications infrastructure (encompassing business processes, application security, application interfaces, and shared infrastructure) supports their overall e-business strategies. The applications infrastructure must be designed so that services such as third-party content or functionality (for example, booking airline tickets) can be integrated in a controlled and secure manner. It must facilitate utilization of standards such that integration among applications or third parties will promote rapid response to market opportunities and leverage investment in technology support infrastructure.

## 6. Technology Infrastructure

The availability, security, reliability, and integrity of services and systems are critical to e-business success. An organization's information technology infrastructure (including networks, data storage systems, computer platforms, system management software, and facilities) must be configured to mitigate the risks in its processing environment as well as to support organizational strategies, which vary by business. For example, a pharmaceutical company's lifeblood is its R&D information, and it is likely to be most concerned with the security of stored and communicated data. On the other hand, an Internet service provider will likely be focused on maintaining continual access to its Web servers. The risks faced by each organization will thus determine infrastructure decisions and priorities.

A disjointed approach to technology creates risks and wastes resources. As organizations drive forward in implementation, many understand the need for directory services infrastructure, without thinking through, at the organizational level, the configuration logic they require today and in the future. They move forward with the implementation of a sub-optimal configuration and

**6. Technology Infrastructure**

*Key Considerations and Strategies at the Technology Level*

| Considerations | Potential Strategies |
|---|---|
| How do we prevent intrusions from the Internet? | Implement, configure, and monitor a firewall, and consider more advanced intrusion-detection systems |
| How available, reliable, and scalable is the IT infrastructure? | Implement redundant and fail-safe hardware and management software |
| Are technology devices properly configured? | Structure an appropriate technology management and audit program |
| Is technology equipment properly cared for? | Provide appropriate systems for safeguarding physical assets |
| Is all this technology necessary? | Structure an appropriate technology management and audit program |

*Figure 9*

are later forced to re-implement. (A simplistic analogy is building software solutions before fully articulating business needs. Sometimes such tactical decisions are called for, as long as they are not confused with strategic decisions.) Corporate culture may also create challenges.

# CONCLUSION

Deploying information assets within an information technology environment creates new and unfamiliar business risks. Organizations must ensure that they are taking sufficient risk in this environment, not just mitigating or controlling risk. Thus, they need to ensure that the e-businesses they develop are supported by a comprehensive risk-management framework that optimizes their new risks—enabling the organization to move ahead quickly.

Properly designed, an e-business risk-management framework can help an organization increase its value in e-space—supporting the development of new products and services, enhancing infrastructure capabilities related to operations and markets, and driving new ways of relating to customers. By ensuring from the outset the security, accuracy, completeness, and integrity of information assets and guaranteeing the reliability and 24/7 availability of processes and transactions, the risk-management framework is an essential strategic component of the successful e-business endeavor. It can also become a critical success factor in the organization's success, enabling it to define and occupy its e-space and attain a competitive advantage within that space.

## ABOUT THE AASC

The AASC (Assurance and Advisory Services Center) is KPMG's center for assurance research and innovation, product development and support, knowledge management and technology tool integration.

## ENDNOTES

[1]"Learn E-business, or Risk E-limination," *Business Week*, March 22, 1999, p. 122.

[2]Gartner, "Information Security Strategies Scenario," a presentation by William Malik offered at the Gartner conference, "Information Security in an E-Business World: Coping with the Threats," New Orleans, June 5-7, 2000.

[3]Jeremy Rifkin. "The Age of Access," *The Industry Standard*, March 13, 2000.

[4]Keyur Patel, Mary Pat McCarthy. *Digital Transformation: The Essentials of e-Business Leadership*, New York: McGraw Hill, 2000, p. 42.

# E-Commerce and Cyber Crime

## New Strategies for Managing the Risks of Exploitation

## HOW ORGANIZATIONS BECOME VICTIMS

Intruders "case" their targets just as other criminals do.[1] They use publicly available information about the technical vulnerabilities of network systems coupled with inside information gathered from unwitting persons[2] to develop attack methods. Both external and internal intruders look for easy-to-exploit weaknesses in their targeted systems or facilities to gain illegal access to them. With the help of specifically trained professionals, organizations can take steps to protect against such vulnerabilities, as outlined in Figure 1.

However, not all attacks begin in cyberspace. Indeed, the physical security of systems and facilities is vital to a proper cyber defense program. (In fact, a fire in an ill-designed facility is as effective, if not more so, in shutting a facility down than, for example, a denial-of-service attack.) Organizations need to ensure

Excerpted from the KPMG White Paper, "E-Commerce and Cyber Crime: New Strategies for Managing the Risks of Exploitation," written and prepared by KPMG's Forensic and Litigation Services Practice and Assurance and Advisory Services Center, KPMG, 2001.

| Attackers look for... | How it creates a weakness | How to mitigate this risk |
|---|---|---|
| ...network computer operating systems, workstations, and other devices deployed in "default" configurations. | A device in a "default configuration" is one that has had little or no reconfiguration to customize it after it left the manufacturer—a frequent practice that provides crackers with a quick and easy way in. | Turn off unneeded services that run by default upon installation on network servers, and ensure that all servers operate with up-to-date security patches to limit exploitation. |
| ..."misconfiguration" of hardware or software, perhaps by activating network services, such as FTP, that have known security issues. | FTP can be used to transfer large amounts of information off of or onto a system. Many FTP server applications have weaknesses that are well known and can be exploited during an attack if they are inappropriately configured. | Design and implement rigorous product selection and testing procedures. |
| ...a "one-size-fits-all" approach to cyber network defense (such as a software-based firewall). | Demonstrates a limited conceptual approach to the complexities of cyber network defense. | Conduct an enterprise-wide architectural security assessment of the domain; create and implement forensic incident response guidelines. |

*Figure 1   Guarding Against Common Risks*

that their physical security systems appropriately control and monitor the comings and goings at their facilities to prevent, for example, an attacker posing as a vendor or service provider from installing unauthorized software on a server to facilitate a subsequent intrusion.

# PARTNERING ALSO CREATES VULNERABILITIES

Businesses often outsource desktop and other Internet-based network support services. Most are also developing e-business alliances and other partnerships with customers, suppliers, and employees—relationships that are essential to e-business. Improperly managed and controlled, however, these new relationships can be as problematic as they are beneficial because, by their very nature, they entrust partial and sometimes complete control of the enterprise's information assets to an outside party.

To verify the professional qualifications and integrity of third-party service providers or potential partners, organizations should consider issues including:

❏ What individuals and entities have ownership interests in the service provider or potential partner?

❏ Is the provider/partner owned or controlled by foreign interests (outside of the host nation)?

❏ What is the cyber security infrastructure of the provider/partner?

❏ In what country are the servers of the provider/partner located (and what are the legal issues associated with that location/jurisdiction)?

❏ What personnel vetting procedures does the provider/partner follow before hiring and exposing its employees to client environments?

❏ Does the provider/partner have contract oversight clauses and an oversight apparatus in place?

## TAKING ACTION TO PROTECT YOUR BUSINESS

E-business security is an ongoing, comprehensive process of adding, removing, and managing layers of actions based upon holistic risk management strategies. In military and other organizations, this concept is now referred to as "defense in depth," a popular moniker that does not capture sufficiently the concept of a "from-the-inside-out" cyber defense.

Because organizations are providing greater access to their systems to both people and systems outside their direct control, they must integrate a cyber defense that encompasses all points of interconnectedness, from the inside out. If they fail to do so, they may leave themselves vulnerable to attacks via, for example, a trusted supplier. Automotive and electronics manufacturers among others, for example, commonly use inventory management systems that make information available to vendors, who then automatically replenish inventory supplies in accordance with established service-level agreements. These systems offer organizations untold benefits—and also pose innumerable risks. Should an attacker gain access to such a system and alter a manufacturer's request for parts in a manner that appears authentic to the vendor, an assembly line can grind to a halt. A cyber defense system must be designed to protect against these and other problems of interconnectedness.

Many organizations, however, have not adapted their security strategies to the inter-connectedness of the electronic world; consequently, they tend to think about security and risk management solutions in a disjointed fashion. They may rely on limited or "one-size-fits-all" strategies such as a particular brand of firewall or a specific means of controlling users or modem deployment. They may favor hardware and software solutions from particular vendors, or take the advice of vendors with whom they have an established relationship in one arena but who may not be qualified to help them with the highly technical specifics of e-crime preparedness.

In the face of escalating e-crime risks, organizations need to avoid one-dimensional, under-informed behavior and, instead, develop a holistic strategy for a cyber defense (see Figure 2).

Leading organizations:

❑ establish clear, focused, integrated security policies
❑ provide employees with appropriate awareness and technical training

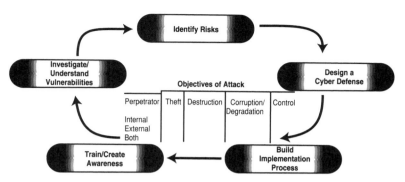

**Figure 2    Helping to Ensure Preparedness**

❑    hire capable, trained workers and support them in establishing and maintaining an integrated response to attacks

❑    instill awareness of electronic threats and risks throughout
the organization

❑    pursue the perpetrators of e-crimes against the organization
to the fullest extent of the law

Such a system offers innumerable benefits both in helping to
deter attacks and in diminishing the effects of an intrusion, should
one occur. Properly implemented and communicated, an enterprise-wide cyber defense system can help the organization prevent
liability on behalf of client management, avert potential lawsuits or
regulatory action, recover lost revenue, and maintain or restore its
reputation and integrity. Preparedness can, thus, become a strategic
advantage in a business environment increasingly dependent on
the security and reliability of computer networks.

## A Good Offense Is the Best Defense

An enterprise-wide cyber defense ideally includes integrated
strategies, established in the form of philosophies, policies, procedures, and practices, and implemented through defined action
plans. Such strategies should encompass technical, legal, and busi-

ness strategies and they should be implemented in a way that considers employees, customers, suppliers, third-party relationships, and other key stakeholders. Thus, rather than a "wrap-around" capability encompassing systems and processes, a strong cyber defense is an integral part of those systems and processes.

In creating a cyber defense, organizational leaders should consider carefully what they have to lose. New-economy business assets encompass a wide variety of intangibles that can be removed with ease in a virtual setting. To understand the implications of potential losses—and to be able to defend against them—organizational leaders need to learn to define "assets" in the widest possible way.

Once organizations know what they need to protect, they need to develop a strategy for implementing an enterprise-wide defense program. Such a strategy must encompass response procedures and standards that are integrated into day-to-day business operations. Cyber defense plans should strike a balance between the demands of accountability of business interests and the privacy interests of employees and customers. The concepts of openness versus security should also be considered in the context of a global electronic environment.

Leaders need to be sure that their business processes accommodate and facilitate a cyber defense. They should also ensure

---

*Assets That Could Be Lost through Electronic Crime Include:*

- banking and financial transactions data
- information related to a business' competitive position
- command and control system data for satellite systems and aircraft
- intellectual property (processes, methods, trade secrets, proprietary data, and other intangible assets)
- litigation-sensitive documents
- personal identification data (whose loss can lead to "identity theft" or stalking)

---

that they have configured the technical architecture of their systems in a manner that complies with and supports the cyber defense architecture. (How they set up and configure how particular transactions will take place, for example, must be consistent with the cyber defense program.) In addition, leaders need to communicate the purpose and value of their cyber defense and assign specific roles and responsibilities for carrying it out. Such a defense plan would encompass:

*Enterprise-wide Planning*

❏ development of a cyber defense infrastructure
❏ integration of human and technical solutions into plans
❏ design and implementation of electronic network intrusion response plans
❏ design and implementation of network monitoring and management plans

*Enterprise-wide Policy Development and Implementation*

❏ use of non-disclosure agreements governing trade secrets, standards of professional conduct for employees, and related issues
❏ policies governing the use of communication systems
❏ policies and action plans to assess the risks as well as the benefits of outsourcing with business partners
❏ policies and action plans tied to assessments of potential civil liability

*Training Programs on E-crime Threat Awareness*

❏ incident response training for all employees
❏ incident response and security training for systems administrators and other technical service personnel
❏ creation and maintenance of forensic incident response guidelines
❏ inclusion of legal and policy issues in annual ethics training sessions for all employees

*A Business Leader's E-Crime Checklist*

Most organizational leaders are familiar with the traditional red flags that could indicate the existence of internal crime. However, e-commerce has changed the shape of business, including the nature and scope of risks. Here are 10 critical questions to help assess how your organization may be at risk for e-crime:

1. Do you have policies and procedures in place for forensic incident response, privacy, and customer management (to mitigate civil exposure)?

2. Do you have a plan in place for communicating these policies effectively?

3. Do you have effective training programs for personnel at a variety of levels, encompassing cyber threat awareness and forensic incident response?

4. Do you have methods in place for vetting potential outsourcing providers?

5. Do you ensure that third-party sources for sensitive technology support are properly vetted as well?

6. Do you perform penetration tests of network systems to correct vulnerabilities?

7. Do you take specific steps to ensure the security of network servers or other systems where intellectual property or other sensitive data are stored?

8. Do you run network intrusion detection systems regularly and have an established plan for following up on the results?

9. Do you run logging functions to record evidence of irregular activities?

10. Do you monitor those network systems on which you deploy banners?

# WHEN THE WORST HAPPENS: AVOIDING FURTHER DAMAGE

When an exploitation occurs, failure to respond or investigate may expose the enterprise and its directors, management, and shareholders to legal and operational risks. Yet, experience shows that many organizations, their employees, lawyers, and technical advisers have little or no understanding or experience in dealing with threatening cyber events. Unintentionally, they often underestimate the intrusion and then fail to take actions that would deter further losses. In other cases, they inadvertently destroy the digital evidence needed to support prosecution, civil litigation, or to provide a basis for administrative action.

Organizations can lose assets in nanoseconds through electronic crimes. When leaders believe that a crime has occurred, they must react instantly, following established forensic incident response plans to minimize further losses, assess monetary and programmatic damages, affix responsibility, and try to recoup losses. The response should include efforts to minimize the organization's civil exposure. To implement such a plan, however, demands an integrated response to the range of legal, technical, programmatic, business, operational, and other issues that are affected by cyber misbehavior.

## Response Personnel Must Have Specific Skills

Today's business leaders recognize the demand for skill sets in the information technology (IT) field. In general, however, IT professionals are trained to set up and provide specific technology services. Typically, they are neither trained nor experienced in dealing with exploitations of those technologies. IT security professionals focus on constructing defensive measures to deal with threats, and some of them are experienced in understanding exploitations. However, very few IT security professionals have the experience and authentic forensic backgrounds to effectively investigate and gather evidence of network-based cyber crimes to be used during the ensuing litigation process.

Cyber investigators must have extensive hands-on experience with and knowledge of computer networks, programs, operating systems, and monitoring tools and practices. Moreover, they must be trained and experienced in the art of collecting, examining, analyzing, and reporting digital findings via a painstaking forensic process to render the evidence admissible in court. Beyond their network and forensics capabilities, investigators must also be skillful at interviewing, knowledgeable about legal issues in various world-wide jurisdictions, and aware of personnel law. They should also be able to act as expert witnesses and interact with the media, should the investigation require it (see Figure 3).[3]

**Digital evidence forensic examinations can help identify:**

- altered accounting records

- altered client records

- digital forgeries

- fictitious, computer-generated documents

- forged documents

- deliberate corruption of business records

- the manipulation of invoicing and payment systems

- unauthorized network system access

**Such examinations can prove:**

- allegations of electronic harassment and cyber stalking

- cyber identity theft

- misuse of enterprise resources

**Such examinations can recover:**

- deleted business information

- evidence of corporate espionage and the use of cyber techniques for the concealment of activities

- inappropriate or offensive e-mails

- secured and password protected data

*Figure 3    Digital Forensics—The Recovery of Evidence*

When responding to attacks, inexperience and lack of knowledge cause businesses to make mistakes that could easily be avoided—and can be devastating in their cost. They include:

❑ allowing untrained personnel to destroy evidence through inappropriate investigations

❑ failing to control information during and after incident detection and response implementation

❑ writing damage assessment reports that inadvertently mitigate losses in favor of the intruder

❑ using "honey traps," "ruses," and other intelligence-gathering methods in ways that fail to protect the respective parties' rights or inadvertently allow an attacker to use the defense of entrapment

❑ misinterpreting criminal laws by failing to seek appropriate counsel

## The New Risks of Civil Litigation Exposure

The use of the Internet as a medium for the conduct of business also poses the risk of civil litigation exposure. The question has become, to what extent is an organization liable for the consequence of damages caused across communications networks by the exploitation or pirating of its point of presence on the Internet? The answer depends on whether the entity exercised "cyber vetting" in developing and implementing appropriate measures to mitigate the risk of cyber misbehavior.

To mitigate civil risks, organizations need to be able to demonstrate that they have developed and implemented adequate policies and reasonable cyber defense measures. Simply put, they need to take appropriate steps to help ensure that their facilities are not used to harm others.

## Legal Systems Lag Behind Technology

Another issue for organizations world-wide is the extent to which cyber crime laws—and perceptions about what constitutes, for example, hacking or other illegal behavior—vary widely across borders. Forensics experts must be knowledgeable about the rules and limitations in each jurisdiction that may be involved in a particular incident.

International protocols are in development; but some experts believe that the seamlessness of the Internet may always require that disputes be resolved on a case-by-case basis. In this uncertain environment, business leaders must be all the more assiduous in working to secure their systems and protect them against further damage if an attack does occur. They must take particular care to understand the relevant laws that apply in the countries in which their servers are located. In addition, leaders must take steps to understand how content providers, service providers (other than hosting companies), and the organization itself could be legally implicated in a forensics situation. They must be aware of the courses of action available should a content (or other) provider's system be used to compromise that of their own organization.

## LOOKING AHEAD: EMERGING RISKS IN A CHANGING BUSINESS WORLD

With the passing of the immediate threat posed by Y2K, the public and private sectors have begun to focus on cyber network defense. Leaders perceive that as technology changes, risks will also change. New technologies will pose new risks and demand new responses to those risks.

In the future, for example, new technologies such as holographic memory, nanotechnology (atomic- and subatomic-level structures), new communications protocols, and other technologies will be introduced and embedded into new core products that organizations will use to facilitate productivity in their infrastructures. Detecting exploitations of these technologies will remain outside the core mission of many organizations—but will require the heightened focus of all organizations. Issues related to the protection and storing of intellectual property developed in a network environment will also create concerns, and cyber protection methodologies will be paramount in this context.

As the technology continues to change, organizations must take steps to understand the related risks that will evolve with technology. They must understand how they might be affected by those risks and ensure that their cyber defense processes and controls are continually updated to meet evolving needs.

## CONCLUSION

The explosive growth of Internet-based open networks paves the way for instantaneous and devastating trans-national electronic crimes that can deny victims the ability to operate their businesses or control their assets. These exploitations will multiply as technologies change, as new technologies are introduced, and as

**Figure 4    Promoting Organizational Preparedness Is a Continuous Process**

intruders' methods inevitably become more sophisticated. Indeed, cyber crime will remain a fact of life for organizations everywhere.

As a result, organizational leaders must take specific steps to defend their assets against electronic crimes with a comprehensive program of training and cyber defense preparedness (see Figure 4). They must also establish a plan for how they will respond should an intrusion take place. (Such a plan offers a wide array of benefits, not the least of which is that it can help enable a successful recovery as well as an effective prosecution of the offenders.) Properly implemented, an integrated program for mitigating the risks of cyber misbehavior can also become a strategic advantage in a world increasingly dependent on the security and reliability of communications networks.

## ABOUT THE AASC

The AASC (Assurance and Advisory Services Center) is KPMG's center for assurance research and innovation, product development and support, knowledge management and technology tool integration.

## ENDNOTES

[1]Intruders learn about their victims by using Internet lookup or yellow page services, X.500 directories, or services running on hosts' machines; reviewing data in public directories; probing mail servers; and using non-network-based data about a victim.

[2]This practice is commonly called "social engineering."
http://www.washingtonpost.com/wp-srv/WPlate/2000-03/02/2141-030200-idx.html

[3]Illena Armstrong. "Computer Forensics: Investigators Focus on Foiling Cybercriminals," *SC Magazine*, April 2000.

# Index

*See also the Glossary starting on page 167.*